IMAGES
of America

CLEVELAND'S
RIVERSIDE CEMETERY

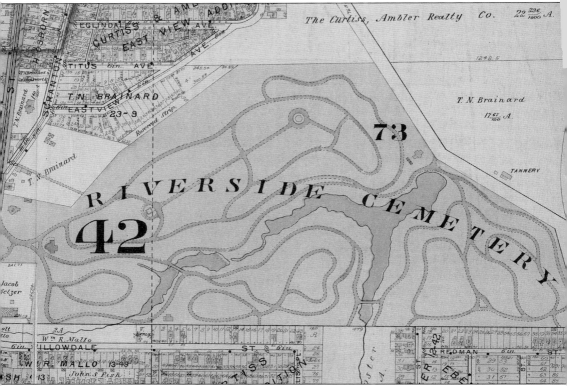

This map from 1898 that shows Riverside Cemetery's location between Jennings Avenue to the east, Pearl Street (later Pearl Road) to the west, and residential lots to the south along Willowdale Avenue also offers perspective of the initial proximity of the Cuyahoga River. The location of the river prior to its restructuring in the 1930s and the ability to stand atop the bluffs within the cemetery overlooking the river gave way to the naming of Riverside Cemetery. This image from the Atlas of the City of Cleveland, Ohio, was published in 1898.

IMAGES
of America

CLEVELAND'S
RIVERSIDE CEMETERY

Jamie Lynne Owens and William G. Krejci

ARCADIA
PUBLISHING

Copyright © 2024 by Jamie Lynne Owens and William G. Krejci
ISBN 978-1-4671-6142-8

Published by Arcadia Publishing
Charleston, South Carolina

Printed in the United States of America

Library of Congress Control Number: 2024933298

For all general information, please contact Arcadia Publishing:
Telephone 843-853-2070
Fax 843-853-0044
E-mail sales@arcadiapublishing.com

Visit us on the Internet at www.arcadiapublishing.com

This book is dedicated to William R. Halley, who gave me my very first "job" by allowing me to tag along with my grandmother Val Craig (a retired administrative assistant) every Saturday to work in the office.

—Jamie Lynne Owens

CONTENTS

ACKNOWLEDGMENTS

Riverside Cemetery has been a place of peace and acceptance from its inception, and because of that, it has become the final resting place for so many of Cleveland's most interesting and influential residents. It is with honor that we find ourselves telling the stories and recording the history of Riverside Cemetery. Special thanks go to William Fredrick Branch, Maria Moldovan, and William R. Halley for their assistance with accuracy and research, the Cleveland Public Library, Brian Meggitt, Aimee LePelley, Mark Tidrick, Curtis Dale Flowers Jr., Angelica Rodriguez, Terry Metter, Michelle Drobik, The Ohio State University, Greg Hatch, Rocky River Public Library, Lisa Sanchez, Karl Brunjes, the Berea Historical Society, Deb Zimmerman, and the staff at Riverside Cemetery. Additionally, we would like to thank our friends and families who offered encouragement and direction during the writing process.

INTRODUCTION

The inception of Riverside Cemetery dates to 1874; however, to better understand the necessity of the large park-like cemetery, it is important to go back a bit further to 1809. Josiah Barber, with his father-in-law Samuel Lord and his brother-in-law Richard Lord, had received a portion of the Western Reserve along the Cuyahoga River. Settling on this land, Josiah was able to promote the expansion of the west side to settlers as well as become the first elected mayor of one of Cleveland's oldest neighborhoods, Ohio City. In a matter of 10 years, Cleveland's west-side population grew by about five times, and by 1870, Cleveland was the 15th largest city in the nation.

Due to the growing population, the need for a large cemetery was expressed by the residents with the hope of establishing something similar to that of the east side's Lakeview Cemetery. At a meeting held on October 21, 1875, at the office of Judge James M. Coffinberry, an association was formed with the purpose of procuring land for a cemetery. The city council felt it necessary to form a committee to work in conjunction with the newly formed cemetery association. With the news that a committee was looking for about 150 acres, many residents were eager to sell their land to the cause. However, the committee had their eyes set on the farm of Titus Brainard as it was believed to be the most beautiful and convenient location within reasonable proximity to the city. Titus Brainard sold roughly 102 acres of his 140-acre farm for $102,457, which the association paid for with the funds raised by the pre-sale of family lots and bonds from Savings and Trust Bank.

On November 15, 1875, an election for the board of trustees and clerk took place. Present at this meeting were Josiah Barber, grandson of former mayor Josiah Barber; J.M. Curtiss; Diodate Clark; John G. Jennings; Samuel W. Sessions; Francis Branch; John Daykin; Robert R. Rhodes; and many other prominent men of the community. Over the next several months, these men began the process of creating budgets, searching for a landscape architect, and discussing salaries for employees. On February 25, 1876, a landscaping contract was signed with E.O. Schwagerl to allow the layout of the cemetery to begin. In April of the same year, they broke ground and Schwagerl's plans were set forth. July 1876 saw the official opening of the cemetery, and an invitation to visit was placed in the local newspaper. In just seven months' time, a substantial amount of work had been completed, which included the construction of an office/cottage and superintendent's home, the Victorian stone chapel and receiving vault, four rustic-style bridges, and approximately five miles of graded roadways. Arguably the most important completed project was the 30 acres of land developed for the sale of family lots and burials.

It was decided by the association that in honor of the country's 100th anniversary and the anticipated success of Riverside Cemetery, a centennial memorial service and tree-planting ceremony be held on November 11, 1876. The celebration was highly anticipated, especially once it became known that the Ohio governor and president-elect Rutherford B. Hayes was to attend since he was in town. The West Side Street Railway Company laid tracks leading right to the entrance of the cemetery for those wishing to attend as well as serving as permanent accommodation for future visitors. Josiah Barber and J.M. Curtiss began the event, each offering a few words, and then introducing F. T. Wallace, who addressed the crowd with a speech in which he expressed great adoration for the cemetery and Cleveland. According to Riverside Cemetery's records of the event, Wallace said, "Probably all great cities have some special points of attraction . . . but in none will there be in all time so much of individual and municipal pride as in Lakeview and Riverside." At the close of his speech, Josiah Barber then invited the Honorable R.C. Parsons to speak, after which all guests headed west down the center road toward the chapel for the tree-planting ceremony. The trees were planted by members of the cemetery association, local business owners, prominent Clevelanders, and Governor Hayes. Governor Hayes, surprised by the large crowd, was not prepared to offer a speech, but just before he planted his tree, he chose to speak quickly of the honor he felt by being there that day. Due to his experience with and appreciation of trees, it was said that the president-elect picked up a shovel, unafraid to dirty himself, and proceeded in such a way that it was clear he must do this often. Two other men who had memorable approaches during the ceremony were founding trustees, Francis Branch and Judge J.M. Coffinberry. Branch, whose health and strength had been declining, completed his planting without assistance. Judge Coffinberry, who had remained in his coach, was "relieved of embarrassment of being crippled" by his wife who planted his tree on his behalf. The ceremony was over once the last groups of trees were planted and the guests began their journeys home. In a report made by J.M. Curtiss about the centennial celebration, he shared his expectations of the future of Riverside, saying, "Let us hope that they (the trees) may abide in decorative beauty long after the hands that set them in place shall be folded in rest, and that when another centennial of our country be celebrated by our children's children, they may rejoice in delightful summer."

The celebrations and ceremonies may have ended at this time, but it was just the beginning of all that Riverside Cemetery would become. In 147 years, there have been several family lots sold, countless improvements to the landscape, and thousands of burials with room for many generations to come. During one of the many meetings in 1875, it was not only a desire but a requirement that Riverside Cemetery remain a humble inclusive burial ground that would continue to serve families for hundreds of years—a practice followed still today with pride and great pleasure.

One

Inception and Development

And now we welcome the new year,
full of things that have never been.

—Rainer Maria Rilke

Riverside Cemetery had its first lots planned and roads laid out in 1876, but it did not end there. Over several decades, the development of the farm-turned-cemetery continued with both major and minor changes bringing the cemetery closer to what it is today. Continued development of unused sections, improvements on the buildings, and general maintenance of the grounds have been topics at the forefront of each superintendent and general manager, all with the same goal in mind: To maintain a reputation that Riverside Cemetery will always have the highest quality of care and consideration for the families who have selected Riverside for their departed family members, caring for each as if an extended member of the staff's own family, and the close attention to and the maintenance of the grounds, always mindful of what the future might bring. It might be fair to say that this chapter may never truly be finished, as the development of future sections has not yet been discussed. The cemetery is also finding a shift in the overall needs of our community and plans to develop accordingly.

RESIDENCE AND FARM OF T. N. BRAINARD, BROOKLYN, CUYAHOGA COUNTY, OHIO. 140 ACRES.

Asa Brainard traveled to Cleveland in 1814 from Connecticut with his son Marvin. Asa acquired 600 acres of uninhabited land from Lord & Barber, on which he built a log cabin and a tavern accommodating those traveling through Cleveland. Over a few decades, the Brainard family sold allotments of their farm. Asa passed away in 1844, and Marvin in 1853, leaving Titus, Marvin's son, roughly 140 acres of farmland to maintain. Titus carried on as a third-generation farmer of a pioneer family until 1875, when he sold approximately 102 acres to the Riverside Cemetery Association. (From *Atlas of Cuyahoga County, Ohio, 1874.*)

Titus Brainard was born in Brooklyn, Ohio, on July 15, 1825, in the log cabin built by his grandfather Asa Brainard. Titus remained on that farm for all 82 years of his life and was well respected by the community. He was known to have been a kind, generous man with good business practices displayed within his agricultural interests. It was within his nature to encourage justice and implement acceptance amongst fellow men. These beliefs became part of the deal when selling his land to the association, saying that the cemetery remains open to all persons, never to be owned by a corporation, city, or church, and maintain reasonable costs so as never to exclude a Clevelander wishing to be buried on his land. (From *A History of Cleveland, Ohio* by Samuel Peter Orth, 1910.)

The farm was filled with small lakes and rivers as well as forested areas and plateaus. The initial planning of the cemetery grounds had worked around these obstacles and attempted to accentuate the beauty of the land. The lakes, like the one seen here, were used for boating and other water activities until it was drained in 1918. (Courtesy of Cleveland Public Library Photograph Collection.)

In April 1876, ground was broken and improvements were made to the Brainard farm. Among these improvements were plans to construct four rustic bridges. Edward O. Schwagerl of St. Louis, Missouri, designed the bridges to allow ease of passing over the ponds, brooks, and ravines. These bridges also offered convenient points of observation at different heights as high as 16 feet. Standing on this bridge is Robert B. Andrews, superintendent of Riverside Cemetery for over 60 years. (Courtesy of Riverside Cemetery.)

Riverside Cemetery's first burial took place on April 14, 1876, with the interment of Margaret "Maggie" Taylor in section 10, lot 125. Originally interred at Monroe Street Cemetery, her husband Matthias heard of the opening of Riverside and made the decision to buy a family lot and have her moved. Maggie's grave remained unmarked for nearly 120 years until Kotecki Monuments provided a nice 12-inch-high marker. (Courtesy of Riverside Cemetery.)

MARGARET "MAGGIE" TAYLOR
FIRST RIVERSIDE INTERMENT

MATTHIAS TAYLOR

Matthias's plans for the whole family to be buried on the family lot were suddenly and tragically changed when he lost his life three years later due to an accident at work. Their two children were taken to New Jersey and raised by Maggie's parents, never returning to Cleveland. (Courtesy of Riverside Cemetery.)

13

SCENE IN RIVERSIDE CEMETERY.

August 4, 1876, the trustees accepted the contract bid of Bruch & Monks to build a Chapel and receiving vault. The trustees wanted a structure within their budget of $4,000 within which Bruch & Monks stayed, accepting two payments totaling $3,855. This initial building had no electricity or heat, exposed stairs and receiving vault, and an open-air ceiling. (Courtesy of Cleveland Public Library Photograph Collection.)

After 20 years, likely finding inefficiencies, architects Steffens, Searles, and Hirsh added the porte cochere and furnace room/coal bin, as well as rooms on either side of the receiving vault with ceilings above the vault stairs and the main ceiling. The north side of the port cochere has inscribed in it a reproduction of a medallion found in the Pere la Chaise Cemetery in Paris, France, that, when translated, reads, "All who pass be silent." The south side of the port cochere has inscribed a downward falling dove with an olive branch in its beak, a symbol of love and peace. The chapel remained open until the final service on June 19, 1953, when it was closed to the public and used for storage until its restoration in 1995. (Courtesy of Riverside Cemetery.)

The success of Riverside called for a more permanent and accommodating office. Charles W. Hopkinson presented his plan of a French Chateau-inspired building, and on July 9, 1896, construction began. Hopkinson's plan called for brown stone that was imported from Massachusetts, a large porch that wrapped around three sides, and a practical interior. The interior held several offices, meeting rooms, closets, storage vaults, and three stunning fireplaces. The gatehouse was equipped with gas lines which allowed for optimum lighting and heat. It still stands today, serving its originally intended purpose, and has been listed in the National Register of Historic Places. (Courtesy of Cleveland Public Library Photograph Collection.)

Shortly after the improvement of the front entrance and the building of the gatehouse, came the addition of the iron bridge. President J.M. Curtiss proposed the 310-foot span to connect the main part of the cemetery with the island plateau in the center of the cemetery. Having once contained a small pond, the area was drained to accommodate Curtiss's new plan for a lawn section. The lawn section only allowed for small gravestones, thus eliminating large family monuments, which Curtiss felt were in poor taste. Planked with a wooden deck, the iron bridge allowed families access to the new section either by carriage or on foot. (Courtesy of Riverside Cemetery.)

In addition to serving as access to the new section, J.M. Curtiss hoped the iron bridge would replace one of the timber bridges, seen in this photograph. The cost for the project was estimated at $16,000 and having just spent $19,000 to construct the new gatehouse, Curtiss called a meeting of the board and pitched his idea with a sense of urgency. The board voted unanimously in favor of the new iron bridge upon hearing Curtiss's plan for smaller lot sections that would appeal to modest purchasers. (Courtesy of Riverside Cemetery.)

With a new bridge, drained ponds, and a plan in place, surveyor John Ackley (left) began planning the leveling and grading of the valley area. The area would serve the purpose of fulfilling the needs of those who did not want traditional, large family lots as well as offering single grave sales for families that did not need to reserve additional graves for future burials. (Courtesy of Riverside Cemetery.)

Temporary train tracks were laid to aid in the daunting task of bringing in dirt to fill in areas as well as transport equipment and workers to and from the job site. It is unclear exactly how long this project took; however, it is known that the largest lake was completely drained by 1918 and the first lots in the lowest valley area were sold in 1922. (Courtesy of Riverside Cemetery.)

A retaining wall was constructed separating section 20 on the upper portion from the steep decline into the valley. Convenient access to the lower half of the cemetery was of great importance since there was only a steel bridge at this time. Therefore, roads were strategically laid in such a way that each new section would be easily accessible by carriage or automobile. (Courtesy of Riverside Cemetery.)

The newly mapped valley sections were complete and ready for sale. A view from the steel bridge, looking northeast into the valley, shows dozens of new trees and an open, green landscape. The lots were mapped out in advance and clay markers stamped with lot numbers were placed to indicate lots sizes. Each lot had a specific number of graves ranging from two to eight graves to accommodate the needs of individuals. (Courtesy of Riverside Cemetery.)

While the house located at the southwest corner of the cemetery grounds was used exclusively as the cemetery's office, another structure was put up on the grounds, immediately to the north of the entrance. In 1875, construction commenced on the Manager's House on Pearl Street, directly across from Dover Avenue, and was completed early the following year. Not long after, stables and a garage were built to the east of this structure. (Courtesy of Riverside Cemetery.)

Manager's house and garage
West 25th Street frontage from gate looking north

Josiah Barber II, buried in section 23, lot 95, grandson of the pioneer settler Josiah Barber, was elected as the first president of the cemetery in November 1875. He served as president until 1880, at which point he remained on the board and served as the superintendent/clerk. Outside of his duties to the cemetery, Josiah was a civil engineer and played an important role in the development of the local railways, including the Cleveland, Columbus & Cincinnati. Josiah passed away in December 1884 and was buried in the family lot he purchased at Riverside. (Courtesy of Deb Zimmerman.)

J. M. Curtiss

Following Josiah Barber II as president was John Milton Curtiss, buried in section 23, lot 105, who served from 1880 to 1916. J.M. Curtiss was a founding trustee and having invested his time into the success of the cemetery felt taking on the position would allow him to see through to the vision he had for Riverside. Curtiss realized the cemetery was in trouble if something did not change quickly so he set out to make improvements. He offered encouragement to the association by sharing his plans to put them in a stable financial situation. His previous business endeavors with the Forest City Nursery and his success with other city expansion projects gave him the skills he needed to make Riverside what it is today. (Courtesy of Cleveland Public Library Photograph Collection.)

John C. "J.C." Dix, buried in section 23, lot 110, served Riverside Cemetery as the superintendent from 1884 until 1916 when he passed away in the home on the property. During his time as superintendent, Dix had impeccable record-keeping skills that have been extremely useful in the office over 100 years later. Dix and J.M. Curtiss worked together to improve and expand the cemetery by offering a variety of sections that would appeal to any person's needs. This all-inclusive philosophy assisted the association with becoming debt-free while also building a perpetual maintenance fund. (Courtesy of Karl Brunjes.)

Robert Andrews, buried in section 10, lot 562, served the cemetery respectfully for 61 years from 1916 until 1977 as superintendent. Upon the death of Dix, Robert Andrews moved into the home on the property where he was able to keep close watch on the cemetery, even stopping some grave robbers on a few occasions. He was known for his reliable attendance and unmatched commitment to his different interests within the community. (Courtesy of Riverside Cemetery.)

In 1930, Martin Ruetenik, who was the president of the trustees, approached Heber Halley (left), buried in section 22, lot 103, to see if he might be interested in the newly available clerk's position, working alongside Andrews (right). Ruetenik and Halley were both associated with an organization called Christian Endeavor and Ruetenik felt Halley would be the perfect fit. Having shown interest, Halley was hired as a clerk and served from 1930 until he retired in 1971. (Courtesy of Riverside Cemetery.)

In 1951, the cemetery needed someone to assist their full-time landscaper, George Szalomka buried in section 5, lot 65, with regular maintenance. Heber Halley's son William R. Halley (better known as "Bill") was in junior high school at the time and accepted the position where he continued to work every available day until he graduated from Baldwin Wallace College. In 1971, when Heber was ready for retirement, Bill (seen here) applied for the position. His nine years of grounds experience and his accounting degree from Baldwin Wallace were desirable by the executive board, and a position was offered. (Courtesy of Riverside Cemetery.)

Every single grave was dug by hand which was a task that Bill Halley participated in during his employment outdoors. When asked what he remembers best about his time as clerk and general manager, he recalls his purchase of the cemetery's first backhoe in late 1974. Perhaps having firsthand experiences of the difficulties, one might encounter while hand digging the graves gave Halley an understanding of the necessity of such an expense. (Courtesy of Riverside Cemetery.)

Bill Halley's greatest accomplishment was the establishment of the Riverside Cemetery Foundation, a 501 (c) (3) account set up to receive tax-deductible contributions to aid in one of the more costly projects the cemetery had seen in a while, the renovation of the Victorian Stone Chapel. In 1987, the chapel was listed in the National Register of Historic Places, and only one year later, in June 1988, ironically on the same day that Robert B. Andrews was laid to rest, the chapel's chimney broke loose and came crashing to the ground. It was a wake-up call to the staff and trustees, prompting Halley to speak with a contractor who warned that without proper restoration, further damage or a loss of the entire building were possible. (Courtesy of Riverside Cemetery.)

Bill Halley began his campaign to raise funds for the intimidating project in 1992, and by the spring of 1995, construction began. From the donations of 163 contributors, all of whose names are displayed on the back wall of the chapel, the entire construction bill of $195,912 was covered. Construction was completed by Platt Construction of Cleveland, a company that displayed first-class craftsmanship, integrity, and dedication. On June 6, 1999, Halley hosted a re-dedication and consecration service celebrating the long-overdue reopening of the beautiful chapel. Then, at an annual meeting of the trustees in November 2009, the members voted unanimously to name the chapel the William R. Halley Chapel in honor of his hard work and dedication to the restoration. Halley considers the chapel his legacy to the cemetery, as it would not be here today if it were not restored. (Courtesy of Riverside Cemetery.)

After Bill Halley's retirement in 2010, the position of general manager was held by Mark Bollinger (2010–2012), Greg Kapcar (2012–2017), and Mark Craig (2017–present), each offering improvements or changes to better the cemetery and ensure the preservation of the historic Cleveland landmark. In 2023, a simple yet necessary improvement was made to the front entrance when new signs were constructed. Craig carefully cut and placed by hand each letter to ensure the longevity of the addition. (Courtesy of Deb Zimmerman.)

Two

EARLY SETTLERS

It is not easy to be a pioneer–but oh, it is fascinating! I would not trade
one moment, even the worst moment, for all the riches in the world.

—Elizabeth Blackwell

Pioneers, whether by trade or travel, have a road in front of them that has yet to be paved. They are the ones who created the cities, towns, laws, and traditions that we either live with today or have read about in history books. If not for the ones who were willing to explore the unknown, there may not be a "Riverside Cemetery" in Cleveland, and perhaps, the land here may look a little different.

Developer, industrialist, judge, and politician, Josiah Barber was born on May 22, 1771, in Hebron, Connecticut to parents Stephen and Alice Cass Barber. He was a partner in the Lord & Barber Realty Company and was responsible for most of the development of Ohio City, where he served as its first mayor. He was a founder and vice president of the Cuyahoga Steam Furnace Company and was appointed a circuit judge in the 1830s. On June 29, 1794, he was married to Abigail Gilbert, who died three weeks after the birth of their daughter in 1797. Five years later he was married to Sophia Lord, the sister of his business partner. Josiah Barber died on December 10, 1842, and was originally laid to rest in a family plot at Monroe Street Cemetery before being removed to section 23, lot 95, with the rest of the family. His remains, along with those of his wife, Sophia, and their children Epaphras, Jerusha, and Sophia were relocated to Riverside on May 18, 1882. (Courtesy of Riverside Cemetery.)

In 1815, Diodate Clark set off on foot to Ohio and had with him just a knapsack and a dollar in his pocket. Upon arrival in Cleveland, he was hired to chop wood and clear land to ready it for new settlers. After a few years of work, he acquired land and continued to do so until he had roughly 200 acres. Diodate became the first male schoolteacher in the city and maintained his interest in the manufacturing industry. (From *Atlas of Cuyahoga County, Ohio, 1874.*)

RESIDENCE of Dr. W. S. STREATOR, Nº 807 EUCLID AVENUE CLEVELAND, OHIO.

RESIDENCE OF DIODATE CLARK, CORNER OF CLARK & COLUMBUS STS. CLEAVELAND O.

He was the first to bring a lime kiln to Cleveland, was an owner and supporter of the Ohio Wooden Ware Company, and served three four-year terms as the county commissioner. He helped the Franklin Street Methodist Episcopal Church break ground and helped organize the first Methodist society on the west side. He helped advocate for the development of Riverside Cemetery and was on the first board of trustees. Diodate passed away in his home in 1876 and is buried in section 28, lot 27. (Courtesy of Deb Zimmerman.)

Seth and Rachel Branch came to Cleveland from Connecticut in 1818. They were fortunate to be close to Josiah Barber, who allowed the family to stay in his home until a cabin could be constructed. Seth passed away in 1825 at 46 years old leaving the legacy of only a home in the woods for his family. Seth and Rachel Branch were buried in Scranton Road Cemetery until Francis Branch moved them to Riverside. (Courtesy of William F. Branch.)

Francis Branch was the son of Seth and Rachel Branch. Francis's brother, John Starkweather Branch, remained at the family home tending to the farm. When John fell ill in 1837, Francis returned to Brooklyn Heights, married Sarah Slaght, and engaged in the duties of farming. Francis was one of the first milk sellers in the area. The edge of the Branch farm gave way to the name of Branch Avenue in Cleveland, later divided by Interstate 90. (Courtesy of Deb Zimmerman.)

Francis Branch held various offices including serving three terms as the county commissioner and was known to have an active interest in all local issues. In 1854, Francis represented Cuyahoga County along with 11 other men at a convention for the purpose of passing a law that would allow freed slaves to obtain equal rights when living in free states. This committee believed that slavery was evil and unfavorable, and it was their duty to make the change. (From *History of Cuyahoga County, Ohio, 1879.*)

SCENE IN RIVERSIDE CEMETERY.

In 1875, Francis Branch joined the committee in charge of securing Riverside Cemetery. He was on the first board of trustees and attended the cemetery's centennial celebration to plant a tree. He had several thoughts and ideas to offer the association about the development of the cemetery, however, he passed away the following year and did not get to see those things through. The monument marking the sprawling 1,800 square feet of burial space is the tallest monument in the cemetery and given its proximity to the entrance of the cemetery, it is likely seen by all who enter. (Courtesy of Cleveland Public Library Photograph Collection.)

Daniel Pomeroy Rhodes, buried in section 20, lot 70, was a businessman in the iron and coal industry. Originally from Vermont and coming from very little, Rhodes settled first in Youngstown where he began his business before permanently settling in Cleveland. Rhodes was also associated with the construction of the Northern Division of the Cleveland & Toledo Railroad. His business endeavors were numerous and seemingly endless. It was with his extensive wealth that he was able to extend kindness and generosity to the needy and less fortunate. After his passing, his wife Sophia Lord Russell Rhodes continued to offer funds to many charitable works. (Courtesy of Cleveland Public Library Photograph Collection.)

Sophia was the granddaughter of the pioneer Josiah Barber. Sophia's father, Robert Russell, passed away in 1837 at the age of 34 prompting Josiah Barber to bring his family from Connecticut to Cleveland. Two years after Sophia arrived in Cleveland, she married Daniel Pomeroy Rhodes, and together, they had three children: Charlotte Augusta (who married Marcus Hanna), James Ford, and Robert Russell. Sophia found interest in devoting her time to charitable works and during the Civil War, she provided for many sick and wounded soldiers. (Courtesy of Deb Zimmerman.)

Charles Halsey was born in 1805 to Asher and Phebe Halsey of Seneca County, New York. Arriving in Cleveland in 1833, he set up a blacksmith's shop on James Street, beside the recently opened Ohio and Erie Canal, and, within a few years, relocated to Columbus Street. In 1834, Halsey married Margaret Stewart, with whom he fathered five children. Margaret died from Bilious Fever at the age of 39 and less than a month later, Halsey married Margaret's 24-year-old sister Jane, who died six months later. The year after Jane's death, Phebe Pryne became Halsey's third wife. Charles Halsey died at the Cleveland City Infirmary of "old age" at the age of 72. Originally buried at Erie Street Cemetery, his remains were moved in January 1909 to Riverside with those of an infant grandson and granddaughter and the remains of his first two wives in section 8, lot 144. (Courtesy of Karl Brunjes.)

Sylvester Lindsley was born on December 17, 1798, in East Haddam, Connecticut, to parents Sylvanus and Abigail White Lindsley. On October 3, 1830, he was married in Meriden, Connecticut to Hannah Andrews, and shortly after, relocated to Ohio. Sylvester and Hannah Lindsley purchased over 90 acres in Brooklyn Township. Later, the land was reduced in size and was bounded by present-day West 65th Street, West 73rd Street, Clark Avenue, and Storer Avenue. Sylvester B. Lindsley died in Brooklyn Township on December 11, 1834. Following his death, his widow returned to Connecticut, where she was remarried two years later and passed in 1857. Originally interred at the old Ohio City Burial Ground near the intersection of present-day Gehring and Lorain Avenues, Sylvester Lindsley was laid to rest beside his one-year-old daughter Hannah, who died on November 25, 1832. Following the closure of that graveyard, their remains were relocated to Monroe Street Cemetery in 1837 and were ultimately moved to Riverside on November 10, 1881, and buried in section 5, lot 59. (Courtesy of Deb Zimmerman.)

Benjamin Beavis was a resident of Cleveland from the age of 10 and is considered a pioneer of the city. He received his education in Brooklyn Township, and in 1851, he was admitted to the bar and commenced the practice of law until his passing in 1884. Beavis was the treasurer of Brooklyn Township, a justice of the peace, and a member of the board of education. In 1871, he was nominated and elected to serve as senator of the 60th General Assembly of Ohio and then elected a second time in 1873. During his time as senator, he played a large role in securing the passage of the bill to build the Superior Viaduct, earning him the unofficial title "Father of the Viaduct." On December 27, 1878, the viaduct opened for traffic and a celebration was held in which Benjamin was appointed and acted as president of that special day. Beavis passed away at 58 years old after dealing a short time with an illness and was buried in section 23, lot 114. His contributions as an early settler, his consideration actions, and his faithfulness for his family, neighbors, and friends were displayed in the overwhelming attendance to his funeral—evidence of his love and high esteem in which he was held by early Clevelanders. (Courtesy of Deb Zimmerman.)

W. H. Beavis.

William H. Beavis, son of Benjamin Beavis and Fredericka Mueller, was born in Cleveland on October 18, 1859. He attended law school at Cincinnati College and in 1883 he graduated with his law degree and joined his father's firm of Beavis & Beavis. Upon his father's passing only one year later, the firm closed, and William still practiced law. However, he also became interested in real estate and several other larger companies for which he held various positions. In 1907, William learned that he had Bright's disease (commonly referred to now as kidney disease) and it was progressing quickly. It is suspected that he was in much pain because, in January 1908, William decided to end his life and was buried in section 23, lot 114. He was only 48 years old, and his wife was not aware of the severity of his condition which caused her to go into shock. Her father, not wanting her to be alone, moved her and her daughter in with him. She was not buried with William, rather she lies beside her father in Lakeview Cemetery. (Courtesy of Cleveland Public Library Photograph Collection.)

Three

MOVERS AND SHAKERS

The purpose of life is not to be happy. The purpose of life is to matter,
to be productive, to have it make some difference that you lived at all.

—Leo Rosten, 1963

A "mover and shaker" could easily be defined as a person who influences change, sparks innovation, or makes grand strides in business. Some of these individuals might challenge societal norms or fight for changes to be made within their areas of passion. Moving or shaking things up too much can sometimes create new obstacles to overcome, therefore finding a balance between pushing boundaries and solving problems is crucial to success and progress. These residents are a wonderful example of what can be achieved when that balance is found. Their hard work, dedication, and fearless tenacity served an important role in writing Cleveland's history and should be remembered by all who may have been affected by their achievements. As Cleveland continues to foster innovation and change, let us remember these men and women for the groundwork they laid. While great effort is being made to promote the accomplishments of those found in this chapter, the research and promotion of those not captured at this time will continue.

JOHN McMYLER,
McMYLER MFG. CO., MANUFACTURERS HOISTING
AND CONVEYING MACHINERY.

Patrick John "P.J." McMyler was a Cleveland native and a member of the board of trustees for Riverside Cemetery. He was active in the oil business and helped establish the National Refining Company. P.J. held the position of director for many oil institutions and was remembered for his wise and thoughtful judgment calls within the business. McMyler was called upon for his advice in regard to combining Lakewood Savings Bank and Cleveland Trust Company, which proved beneficial due to his keen insight being a main factor in the institution's success. He passed away due to heart disease, leaving behind his wife and two children, and is buried in section 23, lot 118. (From *Men of Ohio in Nineteen Hundred*, 1901.)

Carlos Jones, buried in section 23, lot 104, was the founder of the Jones School & Home for Friendless Children in Cleveland. Driven by the loss of his first wife and the loss of his only son, Carlos and his third wife Mary Brainard Rowley Jones established a center to aid children in need. Officers of his corporation included Rutherford B. Hayes, Judge J.M. Coffinberry, Hon. Isaac P. Lamson, and Samuel Sessions. For years, the home operated with the guidelines that only healthy, white, Protestant children be admitted to the home. However, the home dropped those requirements and partnered with several organizations allowing the home to service a broader range of children in need of behavioral health services and counseling. (Courtesy of Cleveland Public Library Photograph Collection.)

In addition to the new partnerships, eliminated acceptance requirements allowed the home to receive funding from places like United Way Services. Carlos and Mary Jones ran their orphanage together until Carlos's passing in 1897. The success of their mission led to the construction of this home in 1902 by architect Sidney R. Badgley. The new building could house up to 75 children and was completed in October 1903. Upgrades were made in the 1920s, 1944, and 1960. In 1997, the Jones Home and the Child Guidance Center merged and operate today as Applewood Centers. The facility stands at 3518 West 25th Street in Cleveland. (Courtesy of Cleveland Public Library Photograph Collection.)

Florence Hohlfelder Oldenburg, buried in section 24, lot 57, was the daughter of Cleveland manufacturer Frederick Hohlfelder and the wife of Dr. Frederick Oldenburg who was the former chief of staff at St. Vincent Charity Hospital. Florence was a founder of both the Cleveland Academy of Medicine Auxiliary and the Women's Guild of St. Vincent Charity Hospital. She held the position of president at both organizations as well as president of the Case Western Reserve Women's Club. Florence followed the philanthropic footsteps of her mother Julia, which Florence exercised by giving both time and money back to the community. She is remembered today as a leader in civic and medical interests. (Courtesy of Cleveland Public Library Photograph Collection.)

Imam Clyde Rahman, formerly referred to as Clyde X, was a leader in and a follower of W.D. Muhammad's Sunni faction of the Nation of Islam and a recipient of a Purple Heart from the Korean War. Imam Rahman was best known for his achievements in both St. Louis, Missouri, and Cleveland, Ohio, although he also led temples in Dayton, Ohio; Dallas, Texas; Kansas City, Missouri; Baltimore, Maryland; and Springfield, Illinois. He was the victim of a shooting that left a bullet in his skull for life and later the target of a bombing to his home in Missouri. Arriving in Cleveland in 1976, he began his work in leadership by helping American Muslims on a pilgrimage to Mecca. In 1983, he helped raise one of the first mosques built by African Americans, the Masjid Bilal of Cleveland located on Euclid Avenue. He encouraged peace and despite how the media portrayed him in the 1950s and 1960s, he spoke out against violence within the Muslim community. He sought to diversify the mosque by hosting interracial activities further inspiring acceptance of all. Despite the racial, social, and religious injustices he faced throughout his entire life, he remained calm and focused. Imam Clyde Rahman is a pillar of strength and perseverance, a role model, and an icon never to be forgotten. After his passing, the Clyde Rahman Community Center was built in his honor, thus allowing his legacy to live on. Imam Clyde Rahman's family buried him in section 35, row 13, grave 51, Riverside Cemetery's natural burial section. (Courtesy of Jamie Lynne Owens.)

Frederick W. Pelton.

Frederick W. Pelton was a trustee of Riverside and served on the board as treasurer. He served as Cleveland's mayor from 1871 to 1873. His work with the Citizens Savings & Loan Associate was the most extensive of his commitments, holding the position of president. He was also active as a Freemason, of which he was a 33rd-degree Mason. He passed away in 1902 and was buried in the family lot in section 28, lot 11. (Courtesy of Cleveland Public Library Photograph Collection.)

Born in New Hampshire in 1861, Harry Farnsworth moved with his family in 1865, settling in Brooklyn Township in 1870. He taught school in North Royalton until 1882, at which time he was admitted to the bar and entered law. In 1917, he was elected president of the newly established Cleveland Metropolitan Parks Board. He married "Bettie" Brainard, a daughter of Titus N. and Clarissa Brainard. He died in 1955 and was laid to rest at the Brainard Lot. (Courtesy of Cleveland Public Library Photograph Collection.)

44

R. F. Humiston

Principal of the Cleveland Institute, Ransom Humiston, buried in section 23, lot 94, was known for his unique and engaging teaching methods. He inspired the students who did not have an interest in schooling and brought a rare enthusiasm to his teachings. Prior to his teaching career, he studied chemistry and geology both locally and abroad and earned an honorary degree of MD at Cleveland Homeopathic College and Western Reserve University. Perhaps the most impressive of his accomplishments is the help he offered to the settlement of a colony in Minnesota. He and a few other Ohioans sought to settle a temperance colony but shortly after an incident that occurred during a Fourth of July celebration, he left town. Humiston is credited for the phrase "Land of 10,000 Lakes" for which Minnesota is known. This credit comes from a speech he delivered at the Minnesota State Fair on September 11, 1874. (From *A History of Cleveland, Ohio, 1910*.)

William Henry Humiston studied at the University of Michigan and Long Island College Hospital. Returning to Cleveland in 1879, he was a member of the surgical staff at City Hospital. In 1892, he was offered a position as a professor at Western Reserve University where he taught until his retirement. He served as president of the Cleveland Medical Society, the Ohio State Medical Society, and the American Association of Obstetricians, Gynecologists, and Abdominal Surgeons. (From *Men of Ohio Nineteen Hundred, 1901.*)

William and his wife would visit Vero Beach, Florida, during the winter. They had fallen in love with the area prompting his purchase of land in 1919. In 1929, he organized the Vero Beach Beautification Society, and in 1937, they took on a project to expand and improve the park. He assisted with improvements until he passed away in 1943. Ten years after his passing, the Vero Beach city council voted unanimously to name the park in his honor. (Courtesy of Virginia McMahan.)

John C. Nokes was an English-born immigrant who settled in Berea in 1866. He had a store on Front Street selling teas and spices. He was a member of the Quarry Masonic Lodge, served as a sharpshooter in the Union army, and assisted with acquiring the first electric lamps in the area. He held the position of mayor of Berea for two terms. He and his wife, Helen, would often travel to Florida to sail their boat. (Courtesy of Berea Historical Society.)

On one such trip, the sail caught a gust of wind and knocked John overboard. Helen jumped into the water to save him; however, he was not brought aboard until nearly two hours later when fishermen approached after seeing her frantic in the water. John's funeral was complete with thousands of floral arrangements, a parade, a singing quartet group, and speeches about his accomplishments. He was laid to rest in section 6, lot 45. (Courtesy of Deb Zimmerman.)

Joseph John Rowe was born in Cleveland on October 3, 1873. In 1900, he was elected a trustee of the Hamlet of Lakewood. When Lakewood became a village on May 4, 1903, Rowe was elected its first mayor. During his term, his administration replaced the old plank road on Detroit Avenue, eliminated the tollgate at Warren Road and Detroit Avenue, and laid out Clifton Boulevard. Following his term as mayor, he served as secretary to US Congressman Theodore Burton and was himself elected to the Ohio Senate in 1920 and 1922. In his later years, he served as a clerk at the board of elections and as a state examiner. Joseph Rowe was married in 1894 to Henrietta May Rauschert, who passed away on November 2, 1934. The following year, he was married to Edna Hilleary. Joseph Rowe died at his home in Lakewood on July 13, 1940, following an illness of more than one year and was buried in section 6, lot 34. (From *Progressive Men of Northern Ohio, 1906.*)

Joseph Poe served as the Democratic representative of Cuyahoga County in the Ohio Legislature in 1874–1875, 1878–1879, and 1884–1885 and fought for fair and equal tax laws. In 1878, he passed a law extending tax deadlines so that families were not forced to pay taxes during the holidays. In 1906, Treasurer Madigan wanted to remove the extension. Joseph was indignant, saying, "A Democrat is trying to undo the product of a Democrat, a Democratic legislature and a law that was enacted under a Democratic governor." (Courtesy of Cleveland Public Library Photograph Collection.)

In 1893, Poe was impeached of his duties on the Democratic County Committee after expressing discontent with their plan to nominate delegates within the committee and campaign for the support of the people. Upon retirement, he sold most of his land to the city for Brookside Park, and the street, Poe Avenue, which was also part of his allotment, was named in his honor. Joseph Poe passed away in 1912 and was buried in section 6, lot 134. (Courtesy of Deb Zimmerman.)

Mason Alexander Hargrave was born in Henrico, Virginia on March 20, 1923, to parents James and Sarah Johnson Hargrave. Raised near Buffalo, New York, he first worked as a waiter but moved to Cleveland in search of new challenges. Not long after his arrival, he took up the mantle of a community activist and ultimately served as president-general of the United Negro Improvement Association. He made his life's pursuit the recognition of the red, black, and green Pan-African flag, which he posted in the rotunda of Cleveland City Hall on February 10, 1984. He passed away in December 1988, and was buried in section 15, row 57, grave 1. (Courtesy of Cleveland Public Library Photograph Collection.)

Richard Revelt, buried in section 39, lot 226, was known as "the Deaf Advocate" due in part to his commitment to the rights of the hearing impaired. At the age of three, Richard contracted spinal meningitis which left him deaf. He was a student at the Alexander Graham Bell School in Cleveland and graduated from St. Mary's School for the Deaf in New York. Revelt took part in a protest in 1982 against CBS for its refusal to offer captions for the deaf and hearing impaired. He organized several deaf and hearing-impaired expositions, drawing in thousands of attendees. He was the chairman of the Cleveland chapter of the Catholic Deaf Association, which aimed to teach hearing people about the needs of those who are deaf. (Courtesy of Deb Zimmerman.)

Born in Oberlin in 1867, Linda Ann Eastman moved to Cleveland at the age of seven. After graduation from West High School, she taught elementary school for seven years before joining the library staff in 1892. Four years later, she took the position of vice librarian and, in 1918, was named director of the Cleveland Public Library, being the first woman to head a metropolitan library system in the United States. She held that position until her retirement in 1938. During her time, she oversaw the construction and opening of the library's main branch on Superior Avenue. She was a founding member and later president of the Ohio Library Association as well as a professor of library science at Case Western Reserve University. (Courtesy of Cleveland Public Library Digital Collection.)

Linda Eastman's work within the Cleveland Public Library system includes her efforts to build the library's Braille collection. She ran into trouble with the high cost of the books and the ability to transport them was another hurdle. By the time of her retirement, the Cleveland Public Library was distributing to 30,000 blind patrons across Northern Ohio. Linda also continued to implement the "open shelf" policy which made the Cleveland Public Library the first large public library to allow patrons to select their own books from the shelves. (Courtesy of Cleveland Public Library Digital Collection.)

Linda received honorary degrees from Oberlin College, Western Reserve University, and Mount Holyoke College. She also received recognition for her extensive contributions to the library system and while Linda's headstone may seem plain and lacking grandeur, her real legacy is within the library system as well as the reading garden dedicated to her outside of the main branch in downtown Cleveland. She was buried in section 9, lot 121. (Courtesy of Deb Zimmerman.)

Dr. Robert Morgan Stecher was a pioneer in the field of rheumatology at Cleveland City Hospital, now MetroHealth Medical Center, establishing the first arthritis clinic in 1935. He was a clinical professor of medicine at Case Western Reserve University, a past president of the Harold H. Brittingham Memorial Library at MetroHealth Medical Center, a former member of the Children's Aid Society, and a founder of the Cleveland Health Museum. He served several other medical organizations in various capacities. (Courtesy of Riverside Cemetery.)

Dr. Stecher was an executive member of the Cleveland Zoological Society since its founding in 1957, and in 1972, the Cleveland Zoo opened its animal care center named in his memory. Dr. Stecher was a collector of documents from Charles Darwin and others within the evolutionary field. When he passed away, his collection was donated and placed in the Stecher Room at the Allen Memorial Medical Library at Case Western Reserve University. (Courtesy of Karl Brunjes.)

W. H. PRESCOTT   —Frank R. Bil

William Prescott was born in 1850 in Somerset, England. At the age of three, his family sailed for the United States, but the ship never completed the voyage. Halfway across the Atlantic, it was wrecked in a storm and the passengers were rescued by a passing ship. Prescott was educated in Cleveland Public Schools and later at Humiston's Institute. In 1874, he was elected Vice President of the Cleveland Dryer Company, a fertilizer manufacturer. In 1899, the company was reorganized as the American Agricultural Chemical Company of New York, to which Prescott served as director and local manager until his retirement in 1923. He was active with the Freemasons and Knights Templar and served as Brooklyn village mayor and president of the Brooklyn Savings and Loan Association. He was married on December 11, 1867, to Sarah Ellen Groff, with whom he had four children. William Prescott died at his Lakewood home, 13954 Lake Avenue, on December 30, 1928, and was buried in section 20, lot 43. (Courtesy of Cleveland Public Library Photograph Collection.)

Born in 1826 in Germany and educated at Berlin and Halle, Herman Ruetenik arrived in New York in 1848 and settled in Pennsylvania, where he was ordained a clergyman of the Reformed Church on July 17, 1853. That October, he was married to Amelia Clara Martin, whose family operated a musical instrument factory in that town. Shortly after, he relocated with his family to Ohio, where he served as a missionary in Toledo and Tiffin. In 1861, Reverend Ruetenik brought his family to Cleveland and became pastor of the First Reformed Church. In 1887, he founded the Eighth Reformed Church and served as its pastor. In his time, he authored no less than seven books on the Reformed faith and established the Central Publishing Company. Herman Ruetenik passed away at his home on Scranton Avenue on February 22, 1914, and was buried in section 11, lot 89. (Courtesy of Karl Brunjes.)

Stephen Buhrer was raised in the Communal Society for Separatists before coming to Cleveland at the age of 18. He worked on the Ohio and Erie Canal and in 1850 established the S. Buhrer Distillery, later called Eagle Distillery, where he built his fortune. Working as a clerk at the commission office next door was a young John D. Rockefeller, and the two became life-long friends. (Courtesy of Barbara Messner.)

Buhrer was elected five times to Cleveland City Council and served two terms as Cleveland mayor, from 1867 through 1871. He was an active Mason and member of the Knights Templar. Buhrer died at his home on Franklin Boulevard in 1907. He was married twice; first to Eva Mary Schneider in 1848, who died in 1889, and next to Marguerite Paterson in 1890. Stephen Buhrer was moved to Riverside in section 23, lot 70, from Monroe Street Cemetery in 1889. (Courtesy of Cleveland Public Library Photograph Collection.)

On May 1, 1868, Mayor Stephen Buhrer purchased lot 42 in Jacob Perkins Subdivision from David and Sarah Sanford at a cost of $3,375. Having hired the architectural firm Griese, Weile, construction promptly commenced on building a fine Italianate/Second Empire home that originally carried the address 327 Franklin Street. When completed later that year, the home was valued at $8,000. It was in this home where the Buhrer family resided until Stephen Buhrer drew his final breaths in 1907. At his passing, Buhrer left over two-thirds of his estate to his second wife, Marguerite, including their home on Franklin. Upon the death of Marguerite Paterson Buhrer in 1914, the house was willed to her brother Abraham, who divided it into a multi-family dwelling and resided in it through the early 1920s. By the mid-20th century, the house had fallen into a state of neglect, but in the 1980s was magnificently restored. Situated in the Franklin Boulevard Historic District at 4606 Franklin Boulevard, it continues to serve as a multi-family dwelling and is a true showpiece of the neighborhood. (Courtesy of Deb Zimmerman.)

Four

CAPTAINS OF INDUSTRY

How wonderful it is that nobody need wait a single moment
before starting to improve the world.

—Anne Frank

Names like Andrew Carnegie, Cornelius Vanderbilt, or John D. Rockefeller might first come to mind when considering a captain of industry. Perhaps lesser known though are the names of the businessmen laid to rest within the gates of Riverside Cemetery. Their efforts to improve and expand the industries with which they were involved are shown through their individual accomplishments. Some of these men laid the groundwork for the increasing popularity of industrial Cleveland by building manufacturing facilities, operating with honor and respect, and keeping the integrity of the quickly developing city at the forefront of their business practices. Some, coming from very little, grew their wealth and chose to donate to various charities and organizations. The impact of their businesses and philanthropic actions has left a meaningful and lasting impression on the residents of Cleveland.

Abraham Teachout and his son Albert established the A. Teachout & Co. in 1873 and sold windows, doors, and other building materials. Their lumber business made Abraham one of the wealthiest men in the 19th century in Cleveland. He cared deeply for the equal treatment of all people, the freeing of the enslaved, and the prohibition of alcohol. The home in which Abraham and his family lived is still standing today at 4514 Franklin Boulevard. Abraham passed away on November 24, 1912, and was buried in section 4, lot 47. (Courtesy of Cleveland Public Library Photograph Collection.)

RESIDENCE AND BREWERY OF C. E. GEHRING, ON BRAINARD, FREEMAN & PEARL STREETS, CLEVELAND, OHIO.

Charles E. Gehring was born on October 2, 1829, in Germany. He immigrated to the United States, joined his brother in Cleveland, and worked at various breweries. In 1857, he established his own brewery on Freeman Street. The C.E. Gehring Brewing Company became one of the most respected businesses in Cleveland and through this concern, Gehring built his fortune. His personal wealth was estimated at nearly $1.5 million. He is buried in section 39, lot 35. (From *Atlas of Cuyahoga County, 1874*.)

Charles William Hopkinson was a Cleveland native who studied architecture at Cornell University and earned his Bachelor of Science in Architecture in 1887. In 1890, he opened his firm in Cleveland. He typically only accepted private, smaller projects apart from Riverside Cemetery's gatehouse, additions to Lakewood High School, and Cogswell Hall on Franklin Boulevard. He was buried in section 10, lot 69. (From *Men of Ohio in Nineteen Hundred*, 1901.)

CHARLES WM. HOPKINSON,
ARCHITECT, SEC'Y CLEVELAND CHAPTER AMERICAN INSTITUTE OF ARCHITECTS.

Christian Schuele was a store clerk for Fries, Klein & Hoover until 1879, when he became a partner. The department store was then renamed Fries & Schuele and operated on West 25th Street. In the 1920s, the Fries family sold their portion of the business and the Schuele family continued to run the store until 1979. Fries & Schuele ran for 110 years and was the second-to-last department store downtown. Charles was buried on his lot in section 20, lot 20. (Courtesy of Riverside Cemetery.)

George Tinnerman, section 22, lot 70, immigrated from Germany with his parents in 1847 at the age of two. Tinnerman opened a hardware shop in 1868 on Lorain Avenue where he sold cast iron stoves and other tools and various items. He felt that he could improve upon the bulky cast iron stove and developed the first steel range in 1875. The steel range stove was extremely successful, and in 1913 Tinnerman closed the hardware store to exclusively manufacture and sell the stoves. (From *Men of Ohio in Nineteen Hundred, 1901*.)

Albert Tinnerman, also buried in section 22, lot 70, was the son of George Tinnerman and the inventor of the speed nut. Originally manufactured as a fastener for the stoves, Albert's son George A. Tinnerman II convinced Henry Ford to use the speed nut for his automobiles. During World War II, the speed nut was used in the production of aircraft for the US government. Albert's invention revolutionized these industries allowing him to build his wealth and expand the family business. (Courtesy of Cleveland Public Library Photograph Collection.)

Production of Tinnerman's stoves was slow at first, as everything was made by hand, and many laughed at George Tinnerman for this idea, believing his invention would rust in 10 minutes. However, the idea was a success, and by 1913, the hardware business was abandoned, and the firm concentrated solely on stove production, becoming a national leader. By 1925, the company was in this large building at 2038 Fulton Road. That year, the company developed an enamel stove but found that the enamel finish would crack due to inadequate nuts that were used in the assembly process. George's son Albert sought a solution to this problem and thus invented the speed nut. By the 1940s, the speed nut business overshadowed the company's stove production, and the name was then changed from Tinnerman Stove & Range to Tinnerman Products, Inc. (Courtesy of Cleveland Public Library Photograph Collection.)

DAVID E. McLEAN,
PRESIDENT THE PEARL STREET SAVINGS & LOAN CO.
PRESIDENT THE HERRMAN-McLEAN CO.

Born on Staten Island in 1856, David McLean came to Cleveland as a boy, was educated in the Cleveland Public School system, and attended Spencerian Business College. He was elected President of the Pearl Street Savings and Trust Company in 1890 and served as a director of the United Banking and Savings Company and as a trustee of the Riverside Cemetery Association. He also held interests in the Fanner Manufacturing Company, Greif Brothers Company, Theurer-Norton Provision Company, and the Rauch and Lang Carriage Company. In 1872, he founded and served as president of the Herrman-McLean Grocery Company, the site of which is now home to the Great Lakes Brewing Company. On May 9, 1881, David was married to Ernestine Teufel. David passed away in 1913 at the Rockwell Springs Trout Club in Castelia, Ohio, following a sudden attack of acute indigestion and was buried in section 28, lot 16. (From *Men of Ohio in Nineteen Hundred, 1901.*)

William Astrup, buried in section 6, lot 30, was a sail manufacturer for ships on the Great Lake beginning in 1876. With sails becoming obsolete, he turned his attention to the production of canvas items and, by 1883, was strictly producing awnings. He designed and patented the retractable awning, allowing him to profit from the parts and hardware in addition to the awnings. In 1956, his company achieved record sales of $10 million with 11 warehouses across the United States and Canada. The old Astrup Awning Company's building still sits on West 25th Street and is home to many nonprofit organizations. (Courtesy of Cleveland Public Library Photograph Collection.)

EDWARD WIEBENSON,
SECRETARY AND TREASURER THE UNITED BANKING
& SAVINGS CO.

Born in 1859, in Prussia, Edward Johannes Louis Wiebenson immigrated to the United States in 1865 with his parents, Jakob and Anna, and younger sister Amanda. First settling in Iowa, Wiebenson attended Rush Medical College and established a drugstore. In 1883, he changed his career, relocated to Cleveland, and accepted a position at the United Banking and Savings Company, where he worked under the direction of his father's friend, Hannes Tiedemann. Over the years, he progressed his way up the ladder, earning the position of president in 1907. He also served as vice president of the Cleveland Pneumatic Tool Company, director of the Beckman Company, Cleveland National Bank, Stark Electric Railroad, and as a trustee of the Public Library Sinking Fund and the Riverside Cemetery Association. Edward was married in 1891, to Dora Louise Tiedemann, the youngest daughter of Hannes and Louise Tiedemann, with whom he had five sons. Edward died from pneumonia following appendix surgery in 1910 and was buried in section 22, lot 140. (From *Men of Ohio in Nineteen Hundred, 1901*.)

On May 12, 1896, Hannes Tiedemann left a letter at the United Savings and Banking Company, where he served as president, allowing Edward to draw upon his personal account, in the amount of four thousand dollars, to build a house immediately to the east of his own residence on Franklin Boulevard. Plans for the Arts and Crafts–style home were laid out by the architectural firm of Steffens & Searles. Construction commenced soon after and was completed the following year. Following the death of Edward, his children continued to occupy the house for another year and soon after, moved out and sold it. Over the years, the house was divided up into a multi-family dwelling. For many years, the house sat unoccupied, but was recently renovated and is located at 4304 Franklin Boulevard. (Courtesy of Deb Zimmerman.)

Forrest A. Coburn, buried in section 3, lot 37, was a senior member of an architectural firm called Coburn & Barnum which was formed in 1878 after Forrest had returned from his studies in New York. Coburn was the head of his firm but also took on the responsibility of secretary of the Civil Engineers' Club and served as an associate member of the Architectural Club. He and his business partner were the architects responsible for the Western Reserve Historical Society Building, buildings for Case Western Reserve University, many Cleveland churches and residences including Coburn's own home pictured here. The mansion, which stands at 6016 Franklin Boulevard, was converted into a duplex and sold in 1912. The home remained a duplex until 1942 when it was converted into an apartment building. In 2002, the mansion was again renovated and currently serves as a four-unit luxury condominium. (Courtesy of Jamie Lynne Owens.)

Martin Snider was born in Dayton, Ohio, on August 16, 1846, the eldest child of Abijah and Martha Lowe Snider. After attending public schools and Dayton Business College, he followed in his father's business of operating a cooperage, or barrel-making company. With the sudden growth of the oil industry, the demand for barrels skyrocketed. In 1868, Snider expanded his operation to Wapakoneta, and three years later, relocated to Cleveland, where he built an extensive plant. In 1878, John D. Rockefeller's Standard Oil Company purchased Snider's cooperage and made him the head of their barrel-making operations, a career he followed until his retirement on his 70th birthday. During his time in Cleveland, he served as president of the Guarantee Title and Trust Company, director of the Cleveland Trust Company, and treasurer of the Riverside Cemetery Association. On November 14, 1867, he was married to Adaline Rohrer, with whom he had nine children. Martin Snider died suddenly on January 1, 1918. Due to frozen ground conditions, his burial was delayed by almost three months, and eventually, he was buried in section 23, lot 101. (From *A History of Cleveland and Its Environs, 1918*.)

Frederick William Stecher was a graduate of the University of Wisconsin where he earned his degree in pharmacy in 1887. In 1901, Stecher had perfected the formula for his Pompeian Massage Cream. He went on to market and sell the product directly to drug stores and barber shops. He advertised with claims to remove double chins and wrinkles while also promoting health and cleanliness. (Courtesy of Cleveland Public Library Photograph Collection.)

In 1904, Frederick William Stecher was president of the Barber's Supply Dealers Association. In 1905, he incorporated the Pompeian Manufacturing Company and began aggressively marketing his product. He added dandruff tonic, night cold cream, face powder, and rouge to his line. Frederick passed away in 1916, leaving his business to his partner Otto Leopold. Frederick was buried in section 22, lot 69. (Courtesy of Karl Brunjes.)

Otto F. Leopold, buried in section 20, lot 19, was hired by Stecher in 1891 to work in his drugstore as a general employee. Over the years, Leopold learned about the cosmetic business, and in 1916, when Stecher passed away, Otto was able to assume the role of president. In 1917, Otto successfully signed movie star Mary Pickford as "Pompeian Beauty of the Year," thus paving the way for the cosmetic industry to become an intricate part of the movie industry. The success of the company was credited to the massive advertising budget, which by 1926 had reached one million dollars. Otto accepted an offer in 1927 from the Colgate Company in New Jersey to purchase the company. Within one month, the Colgate Company moved all supplies, manufacturing equipment, and only a few employees to New Jersey, leaving the majority of Stecher's original employees instantly unemployed and his brand ended. (Courtesy of Deb Zimmerman.)

Martin Ruetenik was born on May 17, 1868, to Rev. Herman and Amelie Ruetenik and at an early age took an interest in agriculture. When he was just 17, he established Ruetenik Gardens on Schaff Road in Brooklyn Heights, where he built his first greenhouse and raised leaf lettuce and tomatoes. In time, he was distributing his produce to multiple states and operating vegetable and Christmas tree farms in Vermilion and Orwell. Around 1901, he inaugurated a profit-sharing plan among his employees and by 1907, had one acre of his Brooklyn Heights operation under glass. At that same time, he helped organize the National Vegetable Growers Association and served two years as its president. He was awarded the Master Farmer prize by the *Ohio Farmer* and served as a member of the Cleveland Farmers Club. Upon the incorporation of Brooklyn Heights, Martin Ruetenik served as its first mayor. He was also president of the Riverside Cemetery Association and of the Lincoln Savings Bank before it became the Pearl Street Savings & Trust. On November 22, 1894, he was married to Katharine Kleinhans, with whom he had 4 children. Martin Luther Ruetenik passed away on September 23, 1947, following a heart attack one week earlier and was buried in section 11, lot 89. (Courtesy of Deb Zimmerman.)

Matthew Bramley was born on January 4, 1868, in Independence, Ohio, to farmers John and Mary Ann Newton Bramley. After receiving a public school education, Bramley entered the paving trade and worked as a teamster and foreman for J.F. Siegenthaler. In 1894, he established the Trinidad Paving Company, which in time grew to become one of the world's largest paving companies, making Bramley a millionaire. In 1910, he purchased Luna Park and in 1917, founded Templar Motors, which produced automobiles in Lakewood until 1924. (Courtesy of Cleveland Public Library Photograph Collection.)

Bramley also served as president of the Land Title Abstract Company and the Cleveland-Massillon Company, and director of the Cleveland Automatic Cleaning Company, Euclid Avenue Trust Company, and the Newburgh Reduction Company. He served two terms in the Ohio House of Representatives between 1898 and 1902. On July 23, 1891, he was married to Gertrude Siegenthaler, a daughter of his early employer, with whom he had four children. Matthew Frederick Bramley died at Lakewood Hospital on May 30, 1941, and was buried in section 23, lot 98. (Courtesy of Cleveland Public Library Photograph Collection.)

Beyond his business dealings and civic involvement, Matthew Bramley also had a passion for yachting. There were three separate occasions related to this that drew much public attention. The first occurred in August 1928 when his yacht *Buddy* was pursued into Rocky River harbor by a Coast Guard cutter who suspected him of smuggling alcohol into the United States from Canada. The next occurred in early 1929, when he purchased the steam yacht *Peary* from Arctic explorer Donald B. MacMillan. That February, he sailed from Boston in search of a sunken island off the California coast, a vision of which had come to him in a dream. After finding the island, he determined that the cost to build and develop it would be too great and abandoned the idea. The following year, Bramley sailed the *Peary* with an expedition to the Yucatan Peninsula to explore Mayan ruins. He later sold the *Peary* to the War Department, who used it as a survey and inspection boat. (Courtesy of Cleveland Public Library Photograph Collection.)

Hannes Tiedemann was born in 1832, in Prussia and immigrated to the United States at the age of 16 with his five siblings and widowed mother. In 1854, he entered the grocery trade and in 1863, he became a cofounder in the wholesale liquor and grocery firm of Weideman and Tiedemann. Tiedemann sold his interests in the grocery firm in the 1870s and turned his attention to investments and real estate ventures. In 1883, he cofounded and served as president of the United Banking and Savings Company, until his retirement in 1907. (Courtesy of William G. Krejci.)

Tiedemann also served as vice president of the Cleveland National Bank, was a founder of the Savings & Trust Company, and was a trustee for Riverside Cemetery. He married Louise Höck (pictured here) in 1862, with whom he fathered six children. The year following Louise's death in 1895, he was married to Henriette Köpcke. He outlived his first wife and all six of their children and died at his home in Lakewood in 1908 and was then buried in section 22, lot 20. (Courtesy of William G. Krejci.)

Regarded by many to be "The Most Haunted House in Ohio," construction of the house that history would come to know as the Franklin Castle commenced in early 1881. Designed by the architectural firm of Cudell and Richardson, the High Victorian Eclectic home was completed between late 1882 and early 1883. The Tiedemann family occupied this home until 1897, at which time they relocated to their summer estate in Lakewood. In 1921, the house came into the hands of a German singing society, which primarily used it for meetings and chorale performances. In 1967, it was sold to the Romano family, under whose ownership stories of a haunting emerged. In the years that followed the Romano's ownership, the house often changed hands and in 1985, was purchased by Michael DeVinko, who had been Judy Garland's last husband. In 1999, it was sold again but was set ablaze by an arsonist. After sitting unoccupied for more than a decade, it was purchased in 2011 and soon after restored. The Franklin Castle is located at 4308 Franklin Boulevard. (Courtesy of Deb Zimmerman.)

John Christian Weideman was born on October 14, 1829, in Lehrensteinsfeld, Württemberg, Germany to parents Johann Christian and Johanna Rosina Rübenkamm Weideman. Immigrating to the United States in 1833, the Weideman family first lived in Philadelphia and New York City before ultimately settling in Medina County, Ohio. John C. Weideman served as president of the Weideman Company and the Forest City Savings Bank and director of the Union National Bank and the Savings & Trust Company. He was a prominent Mason, being active with Bigelow Lodge and the Forest City Commandery. Weideman also served as Cleveland police commissioner from 1876 to 1880, and although approached on the matter many times, he turned down the idea to run for mayor. He was married twice, first to Laura Muntz, on April 17, 1853, who died in 1877, and next to Louise Diebolt, on January 9, 1879. John Christian Weideman died on December 9, 1900, and was buried on his family lot in section 39, lot 53. This image of John Christian Weideman is from *Cleveland und sein Deutschthum*, published in 1898.

In 1846, John Weideman moved to Cleveland and worked for the grocery firm of W.J. Gordon and later Edwards & Iddings. In 1861, he opened his own firm, reorganized it two years later with Hannes Tiedemann, and then incorporated it in 1889 as the Weideman Company. Originally located in the Flats on Merwin Street, and later West 9th Street, the firm grew to become one of the largest wholesale liquor and grocery firms in the United States. It was purchased in 1952 by what would later become Sara Lee Corp. (Courtesy of William G. Krejci.)

Henry Weideman entered the employ of his father's firm, the Weideman Company, where he soon became secretary. Following his father's death in 1900, Henry formed the Weideman Flour Company. He also served as a director of O'Donohue Coffee Company, was an active Knights Templar and Shriner, avid motorist and traveler. Henry married Dorothea E. Burk in 1878, with whom he fathered four children. He died in 1930 at his Lakewood home. (Courtesy of Cleveland Public Library Photograph Collection.)

Born on July 27, 1880, in Cleveland to Ernst and Agatha Leick Mueller, Omar Eugene Mueller attended Cleveland City Schools and continued his education at Harvard, where he graduated in 1903. From 1911 to 1914, he served as American consul in Bahia, Brazil. Following the repeal of Prohibition, he was named president of the Cleveland Home Brewing Company, an establishment that had been organized by his father, Ernst Mueller. He remained in that position until 1945, at which time he stepped down and took the position of board chairman. Omar was otherwise noted as a national champion bridge player, big game hunter, and longtime member of the University Club. He was married to Elsa Weideman, a daughter of John Christian and Louise Diebolt Weideman, on July 8, 1914, and together, they had five children. Omar died from cardiac arrest on June 22, 1946, at his home in Cleveland Heights and was also buried on the Weideman family lot. (Courtesy of Karl Brunjes.)

Ebenezer Fish, a pioneer settler, opened a nursery with J.M. Curtiss, which they ran together for several years. Curtiss brought in Mathias Wilhelmy as a joint business partner. Mathias, having an interest in the business, expanded this established nursery and bought out his partners. He ran his business as a traditional nursery until he passed away in 1903. Mathias's son Albert R. Wilhemy Sr. took over and opened the first storefront called Al Wilhelmy Flowers. The Wilhelmy family is buried in section 5, lot 23. (Courtesy of Deb Zimmerman.)

Otto Konigslow established the Otto Konigslow Machine Company, reorganized in 1894 as the Otto Konigslow Manufacturing Company. Originally building bicycles, the company turned its attention to automotive production and in 1902, released the short-lived but innovative OttoKar. He died in 1932, from accidental carbon monoxide poisoning while working on the engine of his car and was buried in section 6, lot 111. The Otto Konigslow Manufacturing Company continues to operate at 13300 Coit Road. (Courtesy of Deb Zimmerman.)

JOHN EDMONDSON CHAFER,
CHAFER & BECKER, HEATING CONTRACTORS.

John Edmondson Chafer was born in Lawrence, Massachusetts on April 17, 1844, to William and Faith Havercroft Chafer, both of whom were natives of England. At age 10, his family moved back to England, where at age 14, John was apprenticed as an engineer in the railroad shops. He returned to America in 1870 and first worked as a pipe fitter in Buffalo. Two years later, he came to Cleveland and worked as first assistant engineer for the City Water Works. In 1879, he started his own company manufacturing steam pipe fittings, which after several partnerships and reorganizations, ultimately became the Chafer Company of Cleveland. Aside from his primary business, John Chafer also served as President of the Western Realty Company. He was also active with the Masons, Odd Fellows, Royal Arcanum, Builders' Exchange, Cleveland Engineering Society, and the Chamber of Commerce. On August 3, 1864, he was married in Lincolnshire, England to Mary Leah Thorp, with whom he fathered seven children. John E. Chafer passed away on May 12, 1921, and was buried in section 6, lot 176. (From *Men of Ohio in Nineteen Hundred, 1901*.)

Robert Mason Wallace came to Cleveland in 1854 to work with his uncle, the principal owner of Globe Iron Works. He then started his own machine shop, with John Pankhurst and Henry Coffinberry. In 1867, Wallace developed a portable steam engine that improved the process of unloading cargo. They had accumulated enough capital to purchase a controlling interest in Globe Iron Works, which, at the time, only supplied parts to the ship building companies. They purchased a dock nearby under the name Globe Ship Building, and in 1882, they launched the first large iron commercial ship to sail to the Great Lakes. (Courtesy of Deb Zimmerman.)

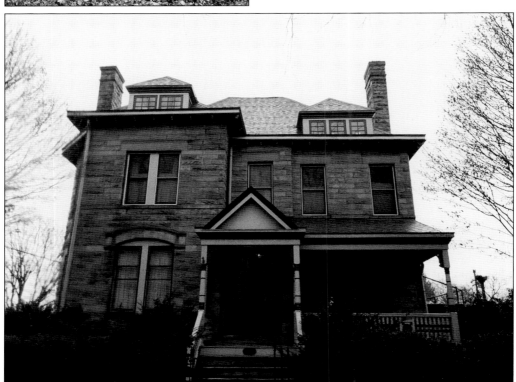

Robert Wallace's fortunes grew rapidly, allowing him and his wife to leave their modest Lakewood home for a mansion on Franklin Boulevard. The home stands today at 4724 Franklin Boulevard and a bed-and-breakfast currently operates from its location. Wallace passed away on March 7, 1911, and is buried in section 22, lot 77. (Courtesy of Deb Zimmerman.)

Five

AMAZING STORIES

*Every man has two deaths, when he is buried in the ground and the last
time someone says his name. In some ways men can be immortal.*

—Ernest Hemingway

Cemeteries offer more than a final resting place. A cemetery holds untold stories, secrets, and family legacies. No matter how significant a story or how impactful one's life may have been, the importance of sharing their journeys is just the same. Visitors to a cemetery may search for famous people whose life's achievements are known by all. Some of Riverside Cemetery's permanent residents have stories that have gone untold for too long or have simply been forgotten. It is important to say these names and both learn from and honor the past regardless of whether the story is good or bad. These are the amazing stories of some of the most interesting residents.

Albert "A.D." Davis Taylor was a landscape architect who is universally known as the first professional landscape architect to practice in Ohio. He established a practice in Cleveland in 1914 and eventually opened a second location in Daytona, Florida. In 1937, he was hired by Cleveland's Mayor Cain and East Cleveland's city manager Charles Carran to design a portion of Rockefeller's Forest Hills Estate. (Courtesy of Cleveland Public Library Photograph Collection.)

Rockefeller Jr. requested a plan that unified city lines and was pleased with A.D. Taylor's 104-page report. Taylor leaves behind his legacy in the contributions he has made to the American Society of Landscape Architects, the editorial work on various books and gardening magazines, and the lectures he gave at several schools. He passed away in 1951 and was buried in section 3, lot 6. (Courtesy of Karl Brunjes.)

Born in 1885, Austin Lloyd first went to work as a lamplighter at the age of nine. The following year, he was employed in a coal mine, and at age 18 was working as a station agent for the Pennsylvania Railroad. He attended The Ohio State University and between 1907 and 1908, played the snare drum for the marching band. During World War I, he served as an engineer with the 4th Infantry Division, primarily building roads and cutting barbed wire fences in France, and was awarded the Purple Heart. Lloyd (left) is pictured with Dr. Prosser in 1908. (Courtesy of The Ohio State University Archives.)

Being the oldest alumnus of The Ohio State University Marching Band, Austin was invited at the age of 95, and again at the age of 100, to stand in and dot the "i" in the band's famous on-field script Ohio. He passed away in 1989, at the age of 103. He was laid to rest in section 28, lot 14, beside Florence P. Lloyd, his wife of almost 70 years, who had passed away in 1988. (Courtesy of Dan Taylor.)

Avery Hopwood was born in Cleveland on May 28, 1882, to parents James William and Jule Pendergast Hopwood. One of four children born to them, Avery was the only one who lived beyond infancy. He attended Cleveland Public Schools and graduated from West High in 1900. The following year, he attended the University of Michigan, where he graduated in 1905. After school, he returned to Cleveland and briefly took a job with the *Cleveland Leader*. A month later, he moved to New York but continued to work as a correspondent for the paper while attempting to get his first play, *Clothes*, produced. Success soon found Hopwood and by 1906, his play was being staged. Known popularly as the "Playboy Playwright," Hopwood's career spanned more than 20 years with at least 25 plays to his credit, including *Fair and Warmer*, *The Demi-Virgin*, and *The Gold Diggers*. In 1920, four of his plays were simultaneously being performed on Broadway. (Library of Congress.)

On the evening of July 1, 1928, while vacationing at Juan-les-Pins, France, Avery Hopwood was swimming with friends when he was suddenly struck with what appeared to be an attack of cramps. He sank before his friends could reach him. Upon recovering his body, they were unable to resuscitate him. His official cause of death was listed as "congestion while bathing." His mother was to meet him there within two days. Three weeks later, the remains of Avery Hopwood were returned to Cleveland and laid to rest at Riverside. A large monument was ordered by his mother, who sadly followed her son to the grave the following March. Upon the death of his mother, by the will of the late playwright, the bulk of his estate reverted to the University of Michigan, where it is awarded to creative writing students through the Avery Hopwood and Jule Hopwood Prizes. Avery Hopwood's father, who died in 1919, is also buried at Riverside but does not take his repose beside his wife and famous son in section 22, lot 120. James Hopwood is buried in section 8, lot 81, beside his children Jessie, Olive, and Eric, who died in infancy. (Courtesy of Deb Zimmerman.)

FEDERAL USA WORK PROGRAM WPA THEATRE

"THE BAT"

A Modern Mystery Play

By Mary Roberts Rinehart and Avery Hopwood

The Thriller That Will Never Die

3 NIGHTS ONLY
THURS., FRI., SAT.
Dec. 10-11-12
at 8:30 P. M.

Grand Street Playhouse
466 GRAND STREET

Orchestra 25c   Balcony 15c

Arguably, one of Avery Hopwood's best and most successful plays, one of the four that ran simultaneously on Broadway in 1920, was *The Bat*. Cowritten with Mary Roberts Rinehart and based on her 1908 novel *The Circular Staircase*, the story was rewritten as a comic mystery, and a villain in a bat costume was added to the plot. New York saw more than 850 performances of *The Bat*, with over 300 being staged in London. It was revived numerous times and even appeared as a novel in 1926. Three film productions were based on it, those being the silent films *The Bat* (1926), *The Bat Whispers* (1930), and *The Bat* (1959), which starred Agnes Moorehead and Vincent Price. The villain in the second film version of the play, *The Bat Whispers*, inspired comic book artist Bob Kane to create his iconic superhero *Batman* in 1939. (Library of Congress.)

MA-KA-TAI-ME-SHE-KIA-KIAH
OR
BLACK HAWK A SAUKIE BRAVE

PUBLISHED BY F. W. GREENOUGH. PHILAD.ª

Among the most noteworthy legends associated with Riverside Cemetery is that of Black Hawk's mother. In 1879, an address given by assistant city solicitor F. H. Wallace claimed that Black Hawk journeyed up the Cuyahoga River in 1883 to Granger Hill, now within the boundaries of Riverside, where his mother was said to have been laid to rest. Accounts from that time contradict this statement and only speak of his visit to Cleveland with Chang and Eng Bunker, the famous conjoined twins. Most likely, Black Hawk's mother is buried near Rock Island, Illinois. (Library of Congress.)

A terrible tragedy occurred on Saturday, June 5, 1926, following an outing of the Theta Tau Theta Society to Northfield. That evening, the members were making their way back to Cleveland in a convoy of four cars when they approached a treacherous railroad crossing on Broadway Avenue in Garfield Heights. Rev. Dr. George Edward Bailey, the 58-year-old pastor of St. Philips Episcopal Church in Cleveland, was driving the lead car. His passengers were his wife, Matilda Sandland-Bailey, age 55, vestryman N. Leslie Sheard, age 33, and Sheard's 55-year-old sister Gertrude Sheard. The driver of the car behind them said that Bailey didn't stop at the tracks before crossing. A moment later, the pastor's car was demolished by a high-speed train on the Pennsylvania Railroad. All four occupants were killed instantly. Their bodies were held in state at the O.S. Spaulding Funeral Parlors on Denison Avenue, with the funeral taking place at 2:30 on the afternoon of June 9 at St. Philips, followed by the interment at Riverside in section 2, lot 228. Three years earlier, Reverend Bailey had built a new church for his congregation at Denison Avenue and West 33rd Street. He was also a personal friend of Theodore Roosevelt. (Courtesy of Riverside Cemetery.)

White House Crossing in Garfield Heights, where this terrible tragedy had occurred, was named for the old White House Tavern, which was originally built as the home of William Billings in 1839. It stood on the north side of the crossing until 1907, at which time it was moved to another location and converted into a barn. The Cuyahoga County Commissioner's Office had worked for years to get the railroad to eliminate the crossing, which had no gates or flashing lights, only guards with lanterns. It was regarded as the most notoriously dangerous grade crossing in the state, with a deadly history going back decades and claiming at least 80 lives. Eventually, people were referring to it as "White Hearse Crossing." The deaths of the Bailey's and Sheard's seemed to have been the straw that broke the camel's back. After years of debate, a plan was soon agreed upon to replace the grade crossing with a bridge. Still, two years would pass before construction of the White House Crossing Bridge commenced. It was finished in October 1929. (Courtesy of Riverside Cemetery.)

Claude Foster was born on December 23, 1872, to George and Julia Schaefer Foster of Brooklyn, Ohio. An accomplished trombone player, he performed with numerous orchestras and bands in the Cleveland area. Most notably, he invented the Gabriel Auto Horn and from this, started his own company and built a fortune worth millions. Upon his retirement, he gave away most of his fortune, roughly $6 million, to various charitable organizations. Foster was married three times, first in 1894 to Emma Schultz, but the two divorced after a few years. He was then married to Lounetta Kelly in 1895, who passed in 1937. The following year, he was wed to Helen Sandberg, who nursed him after he had accidentally shot himself while duck hunting near Sandusky a few years earlier. The two divorced in 1950. He was also the father of two children, Daniel and Earl. Claude Foster died on June 21, 1965, and was buried at Riverside three days later in section 22, lot 201. (Courtesy of Cleveland Public Library Photograph Collection.)

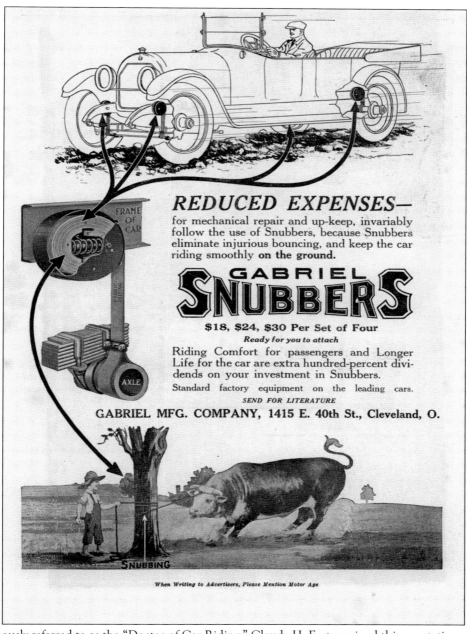

REDUCED EXPENSES—

for mechanical repair and up-keep, invariably follow the use of Snubbers, because Snubbers eliminate injurious bouncing, and keep the car riding smoothly **on the ground.**

GABRIEL SNUBBERS

$18, $24, $30 Per Set of Four
Ready for you to attach

Riding Comfort for passengers and Longer Life for the car are extra hundred-percent dividends on your investment in Snubbers.

Standard factory equipment on the leading cars.

SEND FOR LITERATURE

GABRIEL MFG. COMPANY, 1415 E. 40th St., Cleveland, O.

FRAME OF CAR

FABRIC FELTING

AXLE

SNUBBING

When Writing to Advertisers, Please Mention Motor Age

Famously referred to as the "Doctor of Car Riding," Claude H. Foster gained this reputation as he was responsible for inventing automotive improvements. He first developed his Gabriel Horn in 1904, and the following year, he received his patent. From this, the Gabriel Horn Manufacturing Company was born, which first operated out of the Caxton Building downtown. Improvements to the product were made, and in time, Foster also developed a new automotive shock absorber called the Snubber. The company name was then changed to the Gabriel MFG Co. In this, he developed a profit-sharing program among his employees. In 1925, Foster stepped away from the company, and the name was changed to the Gabriel Company. After falling on hard times, the company closed its doors in 1966. (Courtesy of William G. Krejci.)

Amos C. Cross was born Emil Kriz in Wisconsin in 1860 and moved with his family to Cleveland in the 1870s. Amos was a catcher for Louisville from 1885 until early 1887, at which time he was diagnosed with consumption and released from the team. He returned home where he passed away in 1888. Frank Atwell "Mickey" Cross was born in 1873 and spent almost his entire career in the minors, he played but one game in the Major League with Cleveland in 1901. He died in 1932. Both brothers are buried in section 24, lot 29. (Courtesy of Deb Zimmerman.)

James Ford Rhodes entered the coal business in 1874 with his family, under the name Rhodes & Company. He retired after accumulating a considerable fortune. After retirement, he found interest in American history and writing. He received honorary degrees from Oxford, Harvard, and Yale and his book *History of the Civil War, 1861–1865* won the Pulitzer Prize. James Ford Rhodes High School at 5100 Biddulph Road in Cleveland was also named in his honor. (Courtesy of Cleveland Public Library Photograph Collection.)

James Monroe McClelland was born in Pennsylvania on August 12, 1830, and, in 1861, enlisted as a private with Company B of the 30th Ohio Volunteer Infantry. He was awarded the Medal of Honor for his participation in storming the Confederate Works at Vicksburg in 1863. James McClelland was married three times. He died on April 10, 1915, and was buried in section 13, lot 56. (Courtesy of Deb Zimmerman.)

Christian Narten was born in Germany and, at 17, settled in Cleveland and took a job with the grocery firm Weideman and Tiedemann. Narten ultimately became company president and later, chairman. He married Cora Elise Foote on August 23, 1881. Oddly, both passed away on their 52nd wedding anniversary, only an hour apart from each other, from natural causes. They were laid to rest together in section 39, lot 44. (Courtesy of Deb Zimmerman.)

To say that Henry William Hagert (section 14, lot 9) had a troubled childhood would be an understatement. In January 1942, he was arrested for the theft of three automobiles, sentenced to 11 months at the Industrial Boys School in Lancaster, and released to his parents that December. The following July, his mother had him committed to Cleveland City Hospital, where he was diagnosed with a psychopathic personality, in that he had an emotional abnormality but was not insane. The 17-year-old Hagert was held in the psychiatric ward for a month and was released on August 9. Two days later, Henry Hagert abducted nine-year-old Jack Buchanan with the intention of raping and murdering him. While he did sexually assault the boy, Buchanan's pleas to spare his life had an effect on Hagert. The following morning, he dumped the unconscious boy next to a fallen tree in a field northwest of the intersection of Detroit and Clague Roads in Westlake. After making a series of anonymous phone calls, Jack Buchanan was recovered and taken to St. John's Hospital. Shortly after, Hagert returned to the field, where he encountered a reporter and photographer from the *Plain Dealer*. Their observance of Hagert's odd behavior prompted them to take down his license plate number and pass it along to the police. (Courtesy of Cleveland Public Library Photograph Collection.)

After leaving the field near Clague, Henry Hagert sighted 13-year-old twins James and Charles Collins in front of the Beach Cliff Theatre in Rocky River. They were hitchhiking to Westwood Country Club, where they worked as caddies. Hagert picked them up but drove to Bay Village. He parked at a dead end on Saddler Road, walked the boys into the woods, and shot James Collins (pictured here) once in the back of the head. (Photograph by William G. Krejci.)

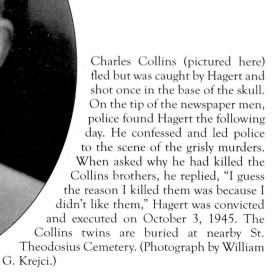

Charles Collins (pictured here) fled but was caught by Hagert and shot once in the base of the skull. On the tip of the newspaper men, police found Hagert the following day. He confessed and led police to the scene of the grisly murders. When asked why he had killed the Collins brothers, he replied, "I guess the reason I killed them was because I didn't like them," Hagert was convicted and executed on October 3, 1945. The Collins twins are buried at nearby St. Theodosius Cemetery. (Photograph by William G. Krejci.)

Born in Cleveland as Charles Mattmueller on February 12, 1878, to parents Karl and Elizabeth Loew Mattmueller, he embarked upon his journey into the mystic arts while still attending West High School. It was then that he first earned his reputation for mind reading and spiritualism. At the age of 18, he set off on a national tour, at which time he adopted the name Karl Germain the Magician, and later, Germain the Wizard. Between 1905 and 1907, he toured Europe and stunned audiences as The American Wizard, spending one year in London at St. George's Hall. He returned to the US and toured from 1908 to 1910, but abruptly vanished from the public limelight soon after. This image of Germain the Wizard is from 1908. (Courtesy of Billy Rose Theatre Division, the New York Public Library Digital Collections.)

Karl Germain, having left the stage, turned his attention to continuing his education. He attended Western Reserve University and graduated with a degree in law in 1914. Not long after, he went into practice as an attorney in Cleveland, a career he followed for many years. In later years, he underwent brain surgery, which led to blindness that resulted in an early retirement. During his final years, he focused his interests on literature, philosophy, and writing poetry. Karl Germain the Wizard died on August 9, 1959, and was buried in section 24, lot 6. For many years, his date of death was missing from his headstone, which seemed to add just one more mystery to his legacy, but in recent years, his date of death was added, bringing a conclusion to that final enigma. (Courtesy of Karl Brunjes.)

Frederick Folberth was born on November 9, 1879, in Mediaș, Romania, to parents Karl and Maria Knopp Folberth. His brother, William Mitchell Folberth, was born on September 24, 1884. Fred came to Cleveland in 1902 and was followed by his younger brother a year later. Both took jobs as mechanics but enjoyed tinkering on the side. In 1916, they invented a carburetor improvement and the following year, started the Folberth Auto Specialty Company. While engaged in a cross-country endurance race, the brothers were faced with the problem of having to clean their windshield with a cloth wrapped around a stick. This led them to inventing the first automatic windshield wiper that utilized wiper blades to clear water and snow from the windshields. It ran off vacuum power that was created by the engine, thus the speed was reflective of how fast the vehicle was running. The Folberth brothers sold their company in 1925 to Trico Product Inc. for more than $1 million, and soon after established the Automotive Development Company, which was responsible for inventing more than 100 automotive devices. (Courtesy of Cleveland Public Library Photograph Collection.)

After selling the Folberth Auto Specialty Company in 1925, William Mitchell "Bill" Folberth joined the Westwood Country Club and took up archery. Having invented his own bow, which incorporated a center slot that made aiming truer, he took the club championship that first year, and was city champion the following. In the early 1930s, he won the Ohio State Championship and, from 1941 to 1945, was the best archer in the United States over the age of 50. In time, Bill Folberth was manufacturing his own improved bows, which earned him the reputation of being "the best bow maker in the world." After living an amazing life, Bill Folberth died on July 21, 1967. He was married to Nettie Carolyn Geist on March 14, 1918, and, with her, had three children. His brother Fred never married. Fred died on September 22, 1955, and both brothers were buried in section 23, lot 203. (Courtesy of Cleveland Public Library Photograph Collection.)

Delta blues legend Robert Lockwood Jr. was born on March 27, 1915, in Turkey Scratch, Arkansas to parents Robert and Estella Stares Lockwood. Following the divorce of his parents, Robert's mother lived on and off with the famed songwriter and blues musician, Robert Johnson until his death in Mississippi in 1938. Robert Lockwood Jr. is the only person that Robert Johnson is known to have ever instructed on the guitar. Robert Jr. started by playing at small house parties and on street corners as a means to support his mother. At just 16 years old, he partnered with Sonny Boy Williamson to record and perform. (Courtesy of Cleveland Public Library Photograph Collection.)

Robert Lockwood Jr.'s music career took him all over the United States, playing with other famous blues artists like B.B. King, Muddy Waters, and Otis Spann. Robert's wife, Annie, purchased him a 12-string guitar that he was not going to use at first but after hearing the beautiful sounds, it became his favorite instrument. In 1960, he and his wife settled in Cleveland, where he was known to play at various clubs including Pirates Cove and Brothers Lounge. Playing music was his passion and he did so until he passed away at the age of 91 and was buried in section 25, lot 200. (Courtesy of Cleveland Public Library Photograph Collection.)

The evening of Saturday, November 16, 1895, was shrouded in a dark and misty fog. At 7:30 that night, Streetcar #642 of the Cleveland Electric Railway was headed south from Downtown, across the Central Viaduct, towards Jennings Avenue, now West 14th Street. The motorman, Augustus Rodgers, briefly stopped the trolley at the approach of the bridge but was signaled by the conductor Edward Hoffman to proceed. What neither could see was that the center span of the bridge was swung open to allow a ship to pass. As it crashed through the gates, motorman Rodgers jumped from the speeding streetcar. A moment later, it plunged 100 feet and smashed against the protective pilings that surrounded the main pier of the viaduct. It then slipped into the river, where it sank and settled under 15 feet of water. Only one man, Patrick Looney, survived the fall. The other 17 passengers were either killed on impact or drowned. (Courtesy of Cleveland Public Library Collection.)

MISS MARTHA SAUERHEIMER.

Martha "Maud" Sauernheimer, age 18, of Merchant Avenue, now West 11th Street, was out shopping in town that afternoon with her 30-year-old sister-in-law, Eliza Sargent Sauernheimer of Professor Avenue. The two were delayed on their return home to Tremont and were aboard the ill-fated streetcar. The remains of Eliza, who was married to Martha's brother John, and had two sons, were recovered shortly after the accident. The body of Martha Sauernheimer was pulled from the river when it was dragged two days later. When approached by a reporter from the *Cleveland Leader*, a member of the Sauernheimer family stated, "This affair appalls us, and we don't know what to do. It seems too terrible to be true. So many people call to express their sympathy, and there appears to be no reality to it. Perhaps we don't yet feel the magnitude of the loss we have sustained." The two women were laid to rest beside each other on November 19 in section 9, lot 169. It should be noted that three more victims of this tragedy are also interred at Riverside. Nearby, one may locate the graves of James T. McLaughlin, age 35, in section 10, lot 333; Minnie C. Brown, age 39, who takes her repose in section 7, lot 46; and Koert Lepehene. (From *The Cleveland Leader*, November 18, 1895.)

Roberto Ocasio was Cleveland's most respected Latin jazz musician. He was a band leader and an educator and promoted Latin music in public schools. He was responsible for the Roberto Ocasio Latin Jazz Camp for high school students. In 2002, he released "Algo Para Ti: Something Just for You" with Little Fish Records. In 2004, when he passed away, the nonprofit Roberto Ocasio Foundation was established to allow his legacy to continue today. Roberto's family buried him in section 30, lot 329. (Courtesy of Deb Zimmerman.)

Mack Henry's grave is marked by a simple headstone on the family lot of Abraham Teachout in section 4, lot 47, though he was not related to the Teachout family. Mack Henry was enslaved throughout the first part of his life, but after gaining his freedom following the Civil War, he went to work for Abraham Teachout as his coachman. Over time, Mack Henry had accumulated over $15,000 in property but remained living with Abraham and his family. Upon Abraham's passing, it was noted that it greatly affected his loyal coachman. Abraham Teachout's widow, Mary, knew that Mack Henry, aged and in feeble health, might not do well with a move and allowed him to remain living with the family in the residence on Franklin Boulevard until he passed away in 1923. (Courtesy of Deb Zimmerman.)

Six

STATUARY AND MAUSOLEUMS

What you leave behind is not what is engraved in stone monuments,
but what is woven into the lives of others.

—Pericles

After the Civil War, a very noticeable change happened when memorializing our dearly departed. Rather than seeing grim skulls, cherubs, and hourglasses, a shift was made to see death in a more positive light. Grief was expected to happen in the grandest of ways, including ornate, large monuments like the ones seen in this chapter. Victorian-era cemeteries will often have the same types of symbols and styles throughout and each symbol had a special meaning to the individual. It wouldn't be uncommon to see pillars, obelisks, urns, shrouds, representations of the seven virtues, and more.

Leonard Schlather was born in Germany in 1834, immigrated to the US with his brother in 1853, and settled in Cleveland three years later. In 1859, he married Katherine Backus and with her had five daughters. Katherine passed in 1890, and in 1897, Leonard married Sophia Schwarz. Aside from his home in Cleveland, Schlather also maintained a beautiful tract of land in Rocky River. (Courtesy of Cleveland Public Library Photograph Collection.)

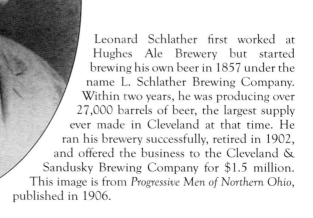

Leonard Schlather first worked at Hughes Ale Brewery but started brewing his own beer in 1857 under the name L. Schlather Brewing Company. Within two years, he was producing over 27,000 barrels of beer, the largest supply ever made in Cleveland at that time. He ran his brewery successfully, retired in 1902, and offered the business to the Cleveland & Sandusky Brewing Company for $1.5 million. This image is from *Progressive Men of Northern Ohio*, published in 1906.

Sophia Schlather was the second wife of Leonard Schlather and 30 years his junior. Sophia was a philanthropist, an art collector, and active within the community. Sophia traveled the world collecting art, books, and other objects, making it to nearly every country. She often donated to the Altenheim Home for the Elderly and the Welsch Home in Rocky River. Sophia had an active role in the Cleveland Day Nursery Association, was a longtime prominent member of the Women's Committee of the Cleveland Orchestra, and held a special interest in the Lakewood Historical Society. When Leonard passed, she honored him by donating $100,000 to the Rocky River Public Library, with which they built the Leonard Schlather Memorial Wing. At her time of passing in 1956, she had $1.9 million to disperse between several charitable and civic organizations including Baldwin Wallace, Lakewood Hospital, Case Western Reserve Society, and the Cleveland School of Art. The Schlather family members were all entombed in the private family mausoleum in section 5. (Courtesy of Rocky River Public Library.)

Joseph J. Cartright was in the lumber business with F.W. Bell, together owning Bell, Cartright & Co., selling doors, furniture, window frames, and other items. Their business ran successfully from 1871 until 1893, when their lumber business took an unexpected nosedive. With the hope that they could make up any debts the next year, the men borrowed $130,000 from two banks but, unfortunately, that did not happen, and the bills had increased. They were ordered to pay back their creditors using their assets. However, they had approximately $1,000 less than needed which meant it was the end of that lumber company. The home in which Cartright's family lived on Franklin Boulevard is no longer standing. It was knocked down in the early 1920s, and the land was sold to the Masons for the purpose of building a Masonic lodge around 1932. J.J. Cartright also served Riverside Cemetery as a member of the board of trustees. The Cartright family is entombed in the private family mausoleum in section 11. (Courtesy of Cleveland Public Library Photograph Collection.)

Born in England in 1836, Thomas Axworthy came to the United States and entered the coal and iron industry. In 1873, he purchased the house at 4206 Franklin Boulevard but eventually built a home on Lake Avenue. Axworthy served as city treasurer from 1883 to 1888. In 1888, he left for London which raised suspicions, sparking an audit of city funds. A shortage of over $500,000 was discovered, which his lawyer partially paid back with Axworthy's assets. (Courtesy of Cleveland Public Library Photograph Collection.)

Coming up $279,000 short, Axworthy pledged to pay back the remainder but never did. He moved to Hamilton, Ontario, where he died in 1893. Still, Axworthy was known as a kind and charitable man, and stories of his philanthropy circulated in the papers following his death. Thomas Axworthy is entombed with his family in their private mausoleum in section 26. (Courtesy of Deb Zimmerman.)

FARM RESIDENCE OF D.S.BRAINARD, SCRANTON AVENUE, CLEVELAND, OHIO—180 ACRES.

David Strong Brainard was born on the family farm in Brooklyn, Ohio on July 27, 1815, to pioneers Ozias and Mary Strong Brainard. He was known to have enjoyed his life as a farmer, never seeking political office, but at the request of friends, served as a Brooklyn Township trustee in 1856 and 1857, and as treasurer in 1845, 1847, and 1863. He is remembered as a kind, honest man and a liberal contributor to the advancement of the city. This image is from *Atlas of Cuyahoga County, Ohio*, published in 1874.

David Brainard married Catherine Prame in 1837 and had four children, two of whom survived childhood, neither producing children. Brainard died in 1880 and a modest monument was set at his grave. In 1889, the family mausoleum was built in section 25, and his remains were transferred. The family surname appears above the entrance with a period at the end, indicating the end of their lineage. (Courtesy of Cleveland Public Library Digital Photograph Collection.)

Cleveland brewer Isaac Leisy passed away suddenly at his Vega Avenue home on July 11, 1892. His funeral was held at his residence three days later and was attended by many friends and admirers. Absent was his son, Otto, who was traveling Europe. Upon receiving word of his father's passing, he immediately boarded a ship and started the voyage home. This photograph shows the Leisy family mausoleum in section 25 which was decorated with copper fittings that matched the red brownstone. (Courtesy of Cleveland Public Library Digital Photograph Collection.)

In 1972, the Leisy family had to make the unfortunate decision to begin the demolition of the family vault. The mausoleum had copper details that were often stolen, and the stones and roof were in disrepair which would have been costly. Rather than continue to make those repairs, the family felt removing everyone and laying them in traditional graves would be a more efficient and cost-effective solution. (Courtesy of Riverside Cemetery.)

After the demolition was completed, the deceased Leisy family members were carefully laid in their eternal graves in a similar position as they were on the shelves in the mausoleum. Being that everyone was together in one mausoleum, there were no individual headstones. The family worked with Kotecki Family Memorials to create identical headstones for each person that would now mark their graves. (Courtesy of Riverside Cemetery.)

The Isaac Leisy Brewing Company was located on 3400 Vega Avenue until it closed its doors in 1958. The Leisy Brewing Company acquired eight acres on Vega Avenue, which allowed it to produce its beer as independently as possible. The most popular beers it had were the Black Dallas malt liquor and Leisy Light, Dortmunder, and Mello-Good beer. When the business closed, it was America's longest-surviving family brewing company. (Courtesy of Cleveland Public Library Digital Collection.)

Dr. William T. Corlett was a dermatologist and was married the Amanda Leisy, Isaac Leisy's daughter. His education was extensive, graduating from Oberlin College, Case Western Reserve University, and the Royal College of Physicians in London. He authored several books, including *The Medicine Man of the American Indian*, and was a teacher, a health board member, and established the department of dermatology in 1898 at Lakeside Hospital. He also served as a consultant in dermatology cases in various hospitals. (Courtesy of Cleveland Public Library Digital Photograph Collection.)

CHARLES RAUCH,
PRES'T THE RAUCH & LANG CARRIAGE CO.; DIR. FOREST CITY
SAV. BK., VICE-PRES'T INDEPENDENT ICE CO., DIR.
FOREST CITY ICE CO., ETC.

Jacob Rauch built carriages in his shop at Pearl and Willey Streets in Cleveland until his untimely death in January 1863. The business was then taken over by his 17-year-old son, Charles. In 1878, Charles Rauch partnered with Charles Lang, establishing the Rauch & Lang Carriage Company. The firm continued to grow and, in 1905, began producing electric automobiles. In 1915, it merged with its competitor, Baker Motors, and operated under the name Baker-Raulang. Their plant still stands on West 25th Street. This image is from *Men of Ohio in Nineteen Hundred*, published in 1901.

In 1867, Charles Rauch was married to Marie Strebel, with whom he had a daughter named Ella. Following Marie's death in 1891, Charles married Katherine Heiss and fathered two more children. The pillared Rauch monument in section 22, lot 97, depicts a broken carriage wheel, signifying the family trade. Charles Rauch, both of his wives, and his daughter Amanda are buried on the lot. His daughter Ella was interred nearby with her husband August Tiedemann's family. (Courtesy of Deb Zimmerman.)

Born in Mansfield in 1818, Judge James McClure Coffinberry came to Cleveland in 1855 and established a legal practice. In 1861, he was elected judge of the court of common pleas and held that office for five years. Known for his clear and direct rulings, none of his cases were ever reversed. Following his retirement, Judge Coffinberry remained active in political dealings. (Courtesy of Cleveland Public Library Digital Photograph Collection.)

Judge Coffinberry was instrumental in establishing a location for Riverside Cemetery. At its dedication in 1876, he was asked to plant a tree. Having been in a recent railroad accident in which he had lost his foot, his wife, Anna Marie, did the honors. The impressive Coffinberry monument in section 23, lot 116, bears the judge's likeness on a bronze plate. (Courtesy of Deb Zimmerman.)

Industrialist Frederick Hohlfelder was a co-owner of the Cleveland Chaplet Manufacturing Company. He also had dealings with the Forest City Machine Works, Cleveland Copper Ferrule Company, Forest City Bedstead Company, the Cleveland Nickel Works, and the Globe Electric Manufacturing Company. Passing away in 1905 at just 42, his family's monument in section 24, lot 57, is topped with a statue of Faith, one of the Seven Virtues. (Courtesy of Riverside Cemetery.)

Bertha Aiken McMyler, buried in section 23, lot 118, was a descendant of Lorenzo Carter, one of the founders of Cleveland, and the wife of P.J. McMyler. After his passing, she spent a portion of her inheritance donating a pipe organ to the Cleveland Museum of Art and set up an endowment of $200,000 to maintain it. The endowment she set up still serves the museum. (Courtesy of Deb Zimmerman.)

The Rhodes family lot is one of the largest family lots within the cemetery located in section 20, lot 70. Spanning nearly 2,000 square feet, the family had plans for many generations to be buried together. Interestingly enough, there are very few burials that actually took place there as most of the descendants of the Rhodes family moved east to Maine and Massachusetts. The remainder of this massive lot will go unused unless anyone from the family decides to come forward and inquire about the burial space. (Courtesy of Cleveland Public Library Digital Photograph Collection.)

SCENE IN RIVERSIDE CEMETERY.

John Daykin was born in England in 1829, the oldest of eight siblings, and came to America with his parents in 1833. In 1852, Daykin came to Cleveland and worked briefly as a stone mason before accepting a position as a brakeman with the Cleveland, Columbus, and Cincinnati Railroad. By 1856, he had been promoted to freight conductor. On April 29, 1865, the funeral train for Abraham Lincoln traveled on the Cleveland, Columbus & Cincinnati Railroad, and Daykin had the honor of being one of the train conductors. He was promoted to passenger conductor, a position he held until his retirement. (Courtesy of Cleveland Public Library Digital Photograph Collection.)

"The Daykin Lion," located on the Daykin family lot in section 23, lot 99, has become a cemetery attraction. It's believed that the lion paid homage to Daykin's birthplace of England. In 1892, John Daykin took his own life. It is believed that ill health brought on such depression that he did not see another way out. Daykin's descendants hope that his story offers light to those who might also suffer from depression and encourage them to seek help. (Courtesy of Ed Miller.)

The massive monument for the Lamson and Sessions families in section 28 features a statue of the Angel Gabriel, passages from Corinthians 15:52 and Psalm 31. The Lamson & Sessions Company was founded by brothers Thomas and Isaac Lamson and Samuel Washburn Sessions, all of Connecticut. Today, it exists as one of the largest fastener companies in the United States. (Courtesy of Cleveland Public Library Digital Photograph Collection)

Thomas Lamson originally worked for the Mt. Carmel Bolt Company and in 1866, partnered with his brother Isaac and friend Samuel Sessions. In 1869, the company expanded to Cleveland and, by 1871, was operating under the name Lamson, Sessions & Co. While moving to a new facility in 1882, Thomas Lamson took ill and died that August. Both he and Samuel Sessions served as founding trustees of Riverside Cemetery. (Courtesy of Cleveland Public Library Digital Photograph Collection.)

ISAAC PORTER LAMSON,
VICE-PRESIDENT THE LAMSON & SESSIONS CO.

Following the death of his brother, Isaac Lamson continued to help the business flourish and greatly affected its prosperity. In 1883, the company was incorporated under the name Lamson & Sessions. Isaac Lamson also served as a delegate to local and national Republican conventions, which afforded him the opportunity to nominate William McKinley for president. This image is from *Men of Ohio in Nineteen Hundred*, published in 1901.

John Gould Jennings married Lillian Lamson, daughter of Isaac Lamson and Fannie Sessions, and served as treasurer of Lamson & Sessions. In 1889, after withdrawing $3,900 for the employees' salaries from the bank, he boarded a streetcar, set the money under his seat, and it was never seen again. Jennings spoke to the papers afterward, indicating that there was no sense of urgency within the company to find the money. (Courtesy of Cleveland Public Library Digital Photograph Collection.)

Herman Junge was a founder of the furniture manufacturing firm Rogers, Billings & Junge. In 1881, a fire destroyed their building and over $80,000 in property. With the firm in ruin, Junge continued on a smaller scale, specializing in upholstered pieces. In 1894, he retired, saying, "I have more than enough to live with and provide for my family. I will spend my days enjoying their company." Sadly, Junge passed away just one year later and is buried in section 5, lot 53. (Courtesy of Deb Zimmerman.)

Dr. Charles B. Humiston was married to Martha Aiken, the sister to philanthropist Bertha McMyler, in 1883 and together they had one son, Hiram Aiken Humiston. Dr. Charles Humiston was a prominent surgeon and physician and was often called to speak during several cases regarding insanity hearings. After an injury sustained to his shoulder in 1893, his work and welfare began to decline. A lawsuit was filed against him in 1895 from the Women's and Children's Hospital in which he had to agree to certain contingencies to avoid a damaging consequence. (Courtesy of Cleveland Public Library Digital Photograph Collection.)

Although Dr. Charles Humiston's days as a surgeon came to an end around the same time as the lawsuit, he still offered expert advice on challenging cases. One such case was that of a 14-year-old boy who received clavicle and vertebrae surgery successfully, which was the first of its kind for that time. By 1903, Martha had filed for divorce on the grounds of "gross neglect." Due to her failing health, the judge expedited the divorce, and within just six weeks and one day she received her divorce. Interestingly, on this family lot in section 23, lot 94, there are 15 recorded burials but only Charles has an individual headstone. (Courtesy of Deb Zimmerman.)

Scottish-born James C. Hay enlisted with the 5th Michigan Volunteers in 1861 and fought in the Battle of Gettysburg. In September 1864, he was honorably discharged. In 1929, he contracted influenza and died a few days later. His monument in section 23, lot 76, is unique to Riverside with its placement of a rifle and swirling smoke, assumed to be a tribute to his participation at Gettysburg. (Courtesy of Karl Brunjes.)

Fred Bloetscher was drafted in 1917 and, the following year, was sent to France. During a German counterattack in the Argonne Forest that October, hundreds of men lost their lives, including Fred Bloetscher. VFW Post 868, which was located on Fulton Road, was named for him. Having fallen into disrepair, the post was sold in 2017 and converted into a restaurant. Bloetscher is buried with his parents in section 3, lot 199. (Courtesy of Deb Zimmerman.)

In 1872, Philip Binz established a monument manufacturing business called Granite and Marble Works. Located at the corner of Riverside Avenue and Pearl Street (now Pearl Road), opposite the entrance to Riverside Cemetery, the site is now occupied by Kotecki Family Memorials. It was said that Binz was a man of rare artistic talent who had the ability to produce both modern and traditional stones. His monument is found in section 4, lot 55. (Courtesy of Deb Zimmerman.)

Born in Connecticut in 1803, Russell Pelton moved to Brooklyn Township in 1835 and established one of the first foundries. In 1839, he helped establish the Brooklyn Academy, a tuition-based elementary school. Denison Elementary School currently occupies the site. Pelton remained intricately involved in his many businesses until his retirement. He passed peacefully in 1888 at the home of his daughter Elizabeth A. Pelton Fish and was buried in section 28, lot 11. (Courtesy of Riverside Cemetery.)

Henry W. Stecher was one of Cleveland's best-known West Side bankers in the early 1900s, holding the position of vice president of the Pearl Street Bank and then the Cleveland Trust Co. after the two merged as well as director of National City Bank. He and his wife, Martha, were involved in many organizations within the city including the Lakewood Garden Club and Clifton Club. (Courtesy of Cleveland Public Library Digital Collection.)

Henry retired in 1933 after accumulating a comfortable fortune and spent the last two years of his life traveling to Florida and going on cruises with his wife. At his time of passing in 1935, his estate was valued at $390,000, which was divided amongst his wife and three adult children. Henry is buried in section 20, lot 52. (Courtesy of Deb Zimmerman.)

Unmistakable and stunning are the graves of the self-proclaimed gypsy families of Cleveland, found in sections 23 and 39. These families typically have grand, heavily decorated monuments and most reference their place within their family. Gypsy funeral services are celebrated with food, drinks, prayer, and fellowship. The love and care exercised by the families for their dearly departed is a testament to the importance of family and culture. (Courtesy of Deb Zimmerman.)

Located in section 39 is the strikingly unique monument of Tom Baran. Baran spent years working with Kotecki Family Memorials to design the monument that marks his future burial location. It captures family and pet photos, illustrations of Jesus Christ, etchings of philosophical thoughts, art, and so much more. Many of his drawings have been donated to the Riverside Cemetery archives so that future generations can enjoy his hard work. (Courtesy of Deb Zimmerman.)

Discover Thousands of Local History Books
Featuring Millions of Vintage Images

Arcadia Publishing, the leading local history publisher in the United States, is committed to making history accessible and meaningful through publishing books that celebrate and preserve the heritage of America's people and places.

Find more books like this at
www.arcadiapublishing.com

Search for your hometown history, your old
stomping grounds, and even your favorite sports team.

Consistent with our mission to preserve history on a local level, this book was printed in South Carolina on American-made paper and manufactured entirely in the United States. Products carrying the accredited Forest Stewardship Council (FSC) label are printed on 100 percent FSC-certified paper.

MADE IN THE
USA